Black Turtleneck, Round Glasses

Expanding Planning Culture
Perspectives

Karin Hartmann

Content

Foreword

In the last three years, the social discourse on equal opportunities for women and other marginalized groups has gained in speed and intensity. It seems as though a tipping point has been reached and the discussion about structural disadvantages has now filtered into the mainstream of society.

Whether it's about gender-care, gender-pay, or the gender-pension gap, the careers of local female politicians, or the disadvantages faced by women in the arts and literature, everyone is talking about the "gender issue."

The number of publications, initiatives, and measures on the subject of equal opportunity has increased in the planning and building industry. The status quo is being uncovered, scrutinized, and discussed. Discriminatory structures in universities and offices are being made public. Publications, podcasts, and illustrated books are explicitly focusing on the forgotten or overlooked work of women planners and architects. Especially on social media, initiatives have emerged and are actively addressing their own content—not just from the perspective of raising awareness about the problem, but proactively and as a matter of course—and forming new networks. This is where the title *Black Turtleneck, Round Glasses* comes in. It evokes associations with Corbusier, Mies, and their coevals, in a way that may tempt us to lapse into a certain nostalgia; but do our heroes still represent today's diverse (architectural) world? Who has a voice, and who is allowed to speak? What is relevant, and who gets to decide? The current debates aim at opening up new perspectives as well as revising old ones. In this instance, the debate is not so much about "adding" in the lived experiences of women, which are largely absent from current perspectives on planning. Instead, it's a matter of adopting an intersectional stance and making it the basis of systemic change in planning culture.

It's even dawning on the mainstream professional discourse, hailing from academia, media, institutions, and firms, that the issue of equal opportunity is not going to automatically be resolved, despite the prevailing openness to solutions. Well-educated women are still missing from the job market, leading to increased pressure to take action and examine the underlying causes. Are there a lack of role models in teaching and in practice? Is the tradition of the profession as it has historically developed not compatible enough? Why aren't women taking up the professional positions they're entitled to?

Now that we've entered a fourth wave of feminism—which is increasingly committed to an intersectional orientation—and a third wave of feminist debates in architecture, it has become virtually impossible to engage in dialog around the professional culture without also engaging in societal discourse.

At issue here is the perspective itself. An environment planned chiefly via a male gaze often disregards the needs of women, whether Black, white, or of color, as well as the requirements of elderly people, children, or those using a baby stroller or wheelchair. What is more, architectural high culture is still defined as the architecture and urban planning that originated in Western industrial nations and which set the perspective of Western thinking as the norm.

In order to understand the views and actions explicitly of women, both in the context of the past and the present, it makes sense to examine the systemic causes of discrimination that have had a heightened effect in architecture, and the impacts of being socialized as a woman.

Black Turtleneck, Round Glasses also addresses the voids resulting from the perspectives that are omitted in architectural planning. What is lost when the lived experience of *others* is missing? Is it possible to establish a causal link between these absent perspectives and a built environment that manifests correspondingly less diversity? Don't we live in a neutral, ready-made city that provides the same backdrop for everyone's everyday life?

Achieving equal opportunity is not simply something that is *nice-to-have* for the industry in Germany or Europe. There are many indications that the reorientation of the entire building industry here vis-à-vis climate change—and, indeed, worldwide—is closely linked to the debate on gender equality. Those courses of action not taken by architects—a practice with a historically androcentric design mindset—as well as the question of who spends what money (and on what), have had a decisive influence on the rather faltering pursuit of climate objectives in recent decades.

In the last few years, initiatives, collectives, and networks have developed, often from within universities, many of them calling for a reorientation of teaching and a professional discourse that embraces diversity. They get along without tradition—and seem to have few points of intersection with "classical professional discourse." Afaina de Jong, the architect of the Pavilion of the Netherlands at the 2021 Venice Biennale, addresses issues of space and society within her work, and in a conversation published in this volume where she discusses her stance on the relationship between activism and architecture.

The professional debate on equal opportunity in architecture is in full swing. May *Black Turtleneck, Round Glasses* contribute to making the discussion and the negotiation processes in planning culture deeper and broader. May a shared love of architecture and a sense of humility toward the privilege of shaping our built environment serve as the common denominator for further development and mutual understanding.

May one-dimensionality turn into diversity!

Young Women and Young Women Architects

"I wasn't a feminist. But after entering the architecture profession, I became one."[1]

Anna Heringer, Studio Anna Heringer

After graduation, architecture students can expect to encounter excellent opportunities on the job market. The industry is booming, and good people are in demand. It's very likely that they will be able to pursue the profession in a fulfilling way, develop their skills, and advance to a leadership position. The trend shows, however, that after entering the profession, the careers of male architecture graduates tend to follow a different path than that of their female colleagues—despite having the same qualifications. Since 2006 more women than men have been graduating from architecture programs. Even so, they are less likely to pursue a career in the profession and more often remain in non-leadership positions. They earn less and are promoted less frequently. In many cases, they turn their backs on architecture altogether in the course of their professional career. Or, alternately, they opt for non-construction architecture-related areas and take up positions in specialist media, foundations, associations, or mid-level teaching. This development, and the prognosis concerning female graduates, increases the professional opportunities that are available for male graduates. Statistically speaking, their female colleagues don't represent much competition. On the contrary, the prospective dropout of women graduates only seems to improve their career prospects.

Why is that? After all, gender equality legislation has been in place for a long time. Although urban planning has been preoccupied with the issue of women architects' invisibility since the 1970s, the effects have remained the same: women architects are less likely to gain a foothold in the architectural profession, often remaining stuck in mid-level positions. While investment in diversifying the STEM subjects (science, technology, engineering, mathematics) is intended

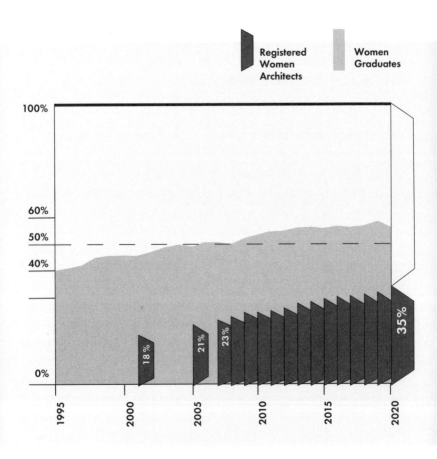

Fig. 1: Women graduates in architecture versus registered women architects 1995–2020
Source: Federal Chamber of German Architects/Federal Statistical Office of Germany H201/ Kaufmann/Ihsen/Villa Braslavsky 2018/Analysis: Karin Hartmann/Infographic: PAPINESKA

to motivate women to study in these fields, keeping them in the profession seems to be an additional problem in architecture.

The Atmosphere in Architecture

According to the 2020 statistics published by the Federal Chamber of German Architects, women make up 35 percent of the country's employed or self-employed registered architects.[2] Only 28 percent of the professorships in architecture are held by women. More than half of women architects, but only one quarter of male architects, work in a non-managerial position, be it in architecture or urban planning offices, public service or business economics.

At the European level, the percentage of women architects has increased in the last decade. According to the Sector Study by the Architects' Council of Europe, the number of women architects in Europe increased from 31 percent in 2010 to 42 percent in 2020. This is an astonishing development, which is chiefly a result of the very high proportion of women architects in Serbia, Croatia, Sweden, and Poland.[3] One percent of respondents described themselves as non-binary or preferred not to comment on their gender.[4]

Structural Disadvantages

According to the study *Frauen in der Architektur* (Women in architecture) by the Technical University of Munich, both sexes are very satisfied with their choice of study and engrossed in their subject.[5] What happens then with the well-educated women university graduates afterward? Time and again, they are hit by a kind of "practice shock" after starting their jobs. It's likely that, like many disadvantaged people in other fields, they experience structural discrimination when they enter the labor market. Very little data is available for Germany and Europe on the extent and systemic nature of structural discrimination against women and marginalized groups in the architecture sector. In North America, there is a great deal more information available. Whereas in Germany the degree of discrimination in the mainstream has been, at best, only partially recognized, in the United States differentiated data on gender- or race/

ethnicity-based patterns of *bias* in architectural practice is now finally available, published in a January 2022 study by the American Institute of Architects (AIA) and Center for WorkLife Law. "A simple definition of bias," the study states, "is when two otherwise identical people are treated differently because of their membership in a social group; indeed, bias is often measured by giving people identical resumes and documenting how people from different social groups are treated differently."[6] Within its 192-pages, the report surveyed 1,346 architects of all ages, positions, ethnicities, and genders, identifying, defining, and analyzing the various *biases* that are found in architecture specifically. The findings are striking and gave the study its name: "We found an elephant in the room: White Men are having a different experience than all other groups in architecture workplaces."[7] In thirteen work areas that were examined—from "Belonging" and "Long-term future" to "Fairness of promotions"—the study identifies the specific disparities that it found between Black men and women, men/women of color, and white men and women.

The study not only provides a detailed account of the grievances in the industry; with the *Bias Interrupters* it also delivers a differentiated instrument for dismantling discrimination and systematically increasing diversity in companies. Evidence- and data-based, these tools offer an easy-to-use working aid through which processes can be structured more sustainably.

The study is a milestone in the architecture industry. It is unparalleled in both its scope and the depth of its investigation. Although the economic, social, and work-culture situation in North American architecture differs from that in Germany, many aspects of professional-culture in the two countries coincide, since they share the same origin—one which applies to and has been adopted across the profession worldwide. The study thus sets new standards and liberates the industry from its state of ignorance. It takes a differentiated approach toward analyzing the working situation of those being discriminated against and gives them options for action—but also arguments for not wanting to work in such a highly discriminatory industry in the first place. The study repeatedly points out that discrimination and *silencing*[8] are preventing the workforce from leveraging its full potential. As a consequence, the best employees work far below their capabilities, to the detriment of the office's profitability.

The comedian Sarah Cooper illustrates how the same statements in the office are valued differently:

Fig. 2: The same statements made by women and men can be interpreted differently

Source: Sarah Cooper/Square Peg London

It will be exciting to see what influence the findings of the AIA study will have on Europe and Germany, where a comparable study doesn't yet exist. In 2020 the Federal Chamber of German Architects conducted a gender-specific survey evaluation of its members. In its analysis of the low percentage of women in leadership positions, the research team Reiß & Hommerich came to the conclusion: "We see, however, that women among the employed members of the chamber, regardless of the length of their work experience, are less likely to be active in managerial positions than their male colleagues. ... The below-average proportion of women active in executive positions ... is *not* attributable to the fact that they possess comparably

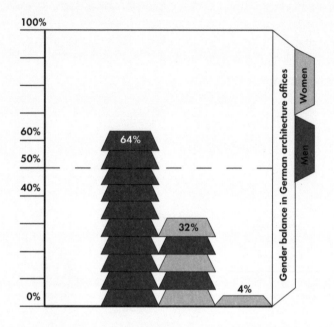

Fig. 3: Gender balance in German architecture offices
listed in the BauNetz Top 100 national ranking
Source: BauNetz Top 100 national ranking, January 2021 /
Analysis: Karin Hartmann / Infographic: PAPINESKA

less professional experience."[9] This statement points toward structural discrimination that, however, was not analyzed in connection with the evaluation. Further evidence of gender discrimination is provided by the Munich study. It reveals the particularly exclusionary professionalization processes embedded in architecture's working culture that may prevent women from advancing to leadership positions: "Women are denied the necessary skills to perform the profession and increasingly relegated to supporting tasks and assistant positions."[10]

Office Structures

An analysis of the BauNetz Top 100 national ranking demonstrates how this uneven gender distribution is reflected in the structures of numerous German architecture firms. A tally of women partners or CEOs led to the following results: out of one hundred firms, sixty-four are entirely led by men. Another thirty-two are managed jointly—but rarely with meaningful gender parity and none with a female majority. Just four firms are entirely led by women. Anyone familiar with the industry doesn't need to think long about which firms those might be.

A *de facto* imbalance is caused by the tradition of liberal professions naming offices according to the surnames of their owners—as such, if a woman is among them, she is not visible at first glance. As a result, when many women firm owners answer their phones, they have to first explain that they aren't the wife of Mr. Smith, but Smith herself.[11] There are, however, several firms owned by women architects that operate under their first and last names, such as Studio Anna Heringer and Helga Blocksdorf Architektur. The architect Gesine Weinmiller has worked under her own name for many years, even though she had a male office partner of equal standing from the outset.

Certainly, it is not a *problem* for women graduates to take their first job in an office with predominantly male management. But it is eye-opening to imagine the inverse, in part because it makes us realize the kind of situation that every male graduate in architecture finds himself in after graduation. For female graduates wanting to learn their trade in a renowned firm, being able to choose from sixty-four offices led by women, and only four by men, is scarcely imaginable. Globally, the situation is not much different. In a 2017 study, the magazine *Dezeen* investigated publicly accessible information on the one hundred largest architecture firms in the world in terms of gender balance. It concluded that the number of women decreases the higher the management level is. Only three of the one hundred firms surveyed were also led by women, though none of them exclusively.[12]

The Self-Employment Alternative

Data from the Munich study suggests that the number of member registrations in the architects' chambers also increases analogous to the rate of women graduates, since there is a time lag in entry into the associations. Unfortunately, there isn't currently any data available at the federal level on chamber registrations broken down by gender. Hence, we are not yet able to analyze whether this trend applies to Germany as a whole and what regional differences, if any, might exist. Nor is there much data on the length of time between graduation and chamber entry. The Munich women researchers' findings revealed a period of five to seven years. Not all of those active in architecture between graduation and chamber entry were included in the Federal Chamber of German Architects' statistics. And chamber admission is—besides its practical importance in conferring architects the authority to present building documents—also a form of qualification and professionalization and thus represents a significant opportunity for career advancement. Moreover, it forms the basis on which architects are accepted into a number of professional associations.[13] In a discussion on the invisibility of women in architecture, Heike Hanada, one of four women architects from the BauNetz ranking, remarked: "You only become visible in this profession when you're self-employed."[14]

A collection of data differentiated by gender would make it possible to investigate chamber admission as a potential structural barrier hampering women and other disadvantaged groups from entering the profession. A study on career progression after graduation would likewise be revealing for both sexes.

Old and New Tasks

"Young women are brilliant. They are brilliant," said British author Laurie Penny in 2015, going on to describe young women as determined, smart, and professional. They have concrete goals and develop good strategies for implementing them.[15] At the same time, many expectations are placed on them. These include getting a good education but also having a family. They are expected to be good cooks and to look good.[16] They are supposed be attractive to men, but not sexually challenging. Because they are girls, they are "protected," and as a result their literal and figurative space for movement is more closely monitored. Their appearance and behavior are commented on from an early age. They are supposed to be relaxed. They are supposed to smile. There is virtually no area of life in which a casual *come as you are* attitude applies for young women. If women fail to successfully realize their education, career, relationship, or to have a child according to schedule, an uptake in concerned inquiries is almost certain to follow. A number of distasteful images of "single women" can be easily conjured. There is little a young woman fears more than the idea of being a single parent.[17] Hence, societal pressures often lead young women to put their own plans on the back burner in favor of securing a partnership at the "right" time.

High expectations are also placed on young men, but these are distinct. They are supposed to be smart, earn a good living, have a career, and at the same time be a caring, present father. Even so, this evolution happens according to a different schedule, and they are allowed to focus on their job and to relax in their free time. Becoming a father for the first time after the age of forty-five is not ideal but, thanks to their statistical tendency to have a younger female partner, it is both biologically possible and socially acceptable. Fatherhood has a different social status than becoming a mother. This is manifest in the societal discrimination against women who are childless and have consciously chosen not to have children. Social approval for young women who, like it or not, decide to give up a well-paying job to take care of their family, and to lend their partner support, is still considerable.

With this sort of socialization in their back pocket—which can, of course, vary a good deal from one individual to the next—women architecture graduates who set foot in an architecture office must *additionally* encounter the professional-culture narratives that have evolved over the course of architecture's history. Even just the image of the always-available male architect who can devote himself entirely to his vocation, and the assumption that architecture can only be done full-time, may lead young women to anticipate that it will be difficult to reconcile family and career in the profession. Currently, women can live better on a widow's pension than on the pension accrued for paid work they perform during their lifetime—assuming their marriage has lasted.[18] This trend will come to an end in a few years since women's employment has increased significantly, as Jutta Allmendinger, president of the WZB Berlin Social Science Center, shows in her book *Es geht nur gemeinsam!* (It can only work together!): whereas the employment rate for women in the German Empire since 1882, and in West Germany until German reunification, was between 35 and 50 percent, it rose to 72.8 percent after 1989. The proportion of employed women has thus almost doubled in a good thirty years. In 2018 it differed only 8 percent from the employment rate for men, at 80.5 percent. Allmendinger sums up: "While little has changed for men in terms of gainful employment in mid-life over the last hundred years, women have massively transformed their lives. They have taken up gainful employment, supported their family financially, and considerably strengthened the economy."[19]

Parallel to this development, however, the distribution of care work has hardly changed. The gender care gap is on average 52.4 percent. If children are living in the household, women perform 83.3 percent more unpaid care work than their partner—which is equivalent to a daily time expenditure of 2.5 hours.[20] The desire for professional self-fulfillment is becoming increasingly important to young women—but often leads them directly into the so-called second shift.[21] If they become mothers, they very likely also take on mental responsibility for all the family's processes, the mental load,[22] a *de facto* second job that in many cases induces exhaustion.

The German government's family policy incentives have certainly supported the institution of marriage for decades, but not spouses themselves in equal measure. In its 2016 study *Mitten im Leben* (In the midst of life), Germany's Federal Ministry for Family Affairs, Senior Citizens, Women and Youth described spousal tax splitting, noncontributory co-insurance coverage, and mini jobs as an "existential threat" for families and as "promoting dependency" for women.[23] After all, and despite all good will, roughly a third of marriages in Germany end in divorce. Or, as the divorce attorney Helene Klaar puts it: "for men, divorce is a financial problem, for women it's an existential one."[24] In this sense, any couple planning to start a family would have to deliberately ignore the family policy incentives, and that for each life decision, in order to make the "right" choice for both spouses in the long run, and to avoid false incentives that may have an effect later down the line.[25]

Becoming a Mother as a Watershed Moment

Against the backdrop described above, be it socialization, professional culture, or family policy, there is much to suggest that planning for motherhood or the birth of one's first child becomes a make-or-break point in the professional biography of women architects. On the one hand, architecture is rather inhospitable for parents with care tasks because of its narratives; on the other hand, they and especially single parents simply no longer have the time for the time-consuming professional hobby of architecture. This realization comes as no surprise in the course of their working lives; instead, it seems to be an implicit part of the professional culture from the outset. According to a 2014 study by *Architects Journal*, 88 percent of women think that being a mother has a negative impact on their career, the same goes for 63 percent of men.[26] In its investigation of the *maternal wall bias*, the 2022 AIA study mentioned above concludes that, contrary to expectations, mothers don't leave architecture because of actual incompatibility. Discrimination toward motherhood plays a major role. Participants in the study were presented with two identical CVs from women, one of which included details of her membership in a parent-teacher organization—revealing, of course, that she was a mother. "The study found very strong levels of bias: the mother was 79 [percent] less likely to be hired, half as likely to be promoted, offered an average of $11,000 less in starting salary, and held to higher performance and punctuality standards."

The gender differences within the *maternal wall bias* are among the greatest within the entire investigation.[27]

Unfortunately, the data for Germany is also very sparse in this area. In this respect, too, it would be interesting to know how many women architects in Germany have either consciously or unconsciously chosen not to have children simply because reconciling motherhood with their career didn't seem possible.[28] If the overall situation regarding maternity is at all similar to that in North America, there is an urgent need for action here.

The Part-Time Box

With its cultivated culture of presence and its narrative of constant availability, architecture seems to be virtually a zero-tolerance zone when it comes to accepting part-time employment. Studies consistently show that part-time employees are paid and promoted less. They're also given tasks with less responsibility.[29] For women, part-time work thus becomes a downward spiral and, as a consequence, may even become a subtle career killer. For many women employed as architects who do have children, this means that they're multiply punished. They earn less money, are given less responsibility, and have very little chance of being promoted. At the same time, they are expected to work overtime on the job for the sake of an important cause—while at home they have to attend to care work that can't be postponed. If these conditions coincide with the family policy incentives mentioned above, such as spousal tax splitting, the hard-won time in the planning office becomes a *de facto* hobby that doesn't pay off in the long run. This is not only frustrating, but in fact doesn't represent a professional perspective, especially given that with the onset of motherhood, it seems the ship of "architecture-as-vocation" has sailed for good. This presence-and-overtime culture is particularly pronounced in Germany; the Scandinavian countries could serve as a model for a good work-life balance.[30]

The Janus-faced nature of the industry's reluctance to allow employees to balance part-time work alongside caring responsibilities becomes particularly obvious when a partner in a firm takes on a professorship. It is indeed possible to work part-time, it simply depends on the reason.

The bias against mothers is obsolete. It overlooks how effectively people with care responsibilities can work part-time, how well they are trained, and the enriched perspective they bring to planning. In contrast to their full-time colleagues, they are certain to encounter many more diverse situations in their day-to-day lives. Where is diversity supposed to come from in a professional culture that monopolizes the private lives of planners to the point of asceticism? Canadian geography professor and author of the book *Feminist City*, Leslie Kern, explains that women often experience the city as a series of physical, social, economic, and symbolic hurdles that impair their everyday life. "Many of these barriers are invisible to men, because their own set of experiences means they rarely encounter them."[31] Taken to its logical conclusion, upholding limiting beliefs in professional culture also means that, unfortunately, interesting alternative approaches beyond full-time work—such as networks and offices of mothers working together, or deceleration movements like Mette Aamodt's Slow Architecture[32] as well as many New Work innovations—remain under the industry's radar. Margit Sichrovsky, co-owner of the woman-led architecture office LXSY Architekten in Berlin, has commented on this in a podcast, saying that when she founded the office with her partner Kim Le Roux, the focus was on choosing and designing their own working environment.[33]

The Limits of Childcare

One of the reasons why women are less able and willing to work is due to insufficient childcare. In her book *The Double X Economy*, Linda Scott points out how the offer of free, high-quality childcare pays for itself in just a few years. This is because the prospective taxes generated by women would be considerably higher than the cost of childcare.[34] She demonstrates how the Western world regards children as a private luxury, suggesting that: "For instance, the rich nations' failure to invest in childcare forces millions of women who prefer full-time jobs to work part-time or quit completely, leaving billions in GDP on the table."[35] Scott elaborates how much is invested in the education of these women through family savings, state grants and stipends, university donations and taxpayers' money, while on the other hand there is a shortage of highly qualified workers.[36] Women's demands for good, nurturing childcare are justified: as the parent who is often *de facto* responsible for the child's development, they are only satisfied when the level of care is very good. All in all, this is a responsible attitude that benefits society as a whole. As Scott sums up: "Of all the policies and programs intended to support working mothers, sponsored childcare is the only thing proven to work."[37] Ironically, it is also precisely this policy that has kept successful full-time fathers in the architecture industry safe for decades through the government-subsidized breadwinner model—which allows a woman to remain at home and take care of everything. That is exactly what women want to be able to work "in peace." The industry's claim on men's availability thus creates a shortage—that is, of women—that is felt across the industry itself.[38] This question cannot be solved without questioning the culture of presence itself. Is the work of architects really so time-consuming or is this an aspect that the sector in fact anticipates?[39] The industry would do well to challenge these "norms" and to support caregivers in any way it can, whether in the form of company kindergartens or by offering greater flexibility.

Individual Decisions

In the study *Frauen in der Architektur* (Women in architecture) many of the interviews suggest that women "don't want to," "don't want to overextend" themselves, et cetera. Yet such viewpoints leave women architects and other marginalized groups to fend for themselves and contend against their own doubts. As Katharina Weresch points out in her article "Rund um die Uhr gefordert" (On demand around the clock) in the *Deutsches Architektenblatt*, women architects see themselves confronted with a personal conflict as a result of the processes laid out above, which they then have to resolve alone: "This individualization is wrong; it is a societal problem that we all have to solve."[40]

One of the first studies of its kind, "Why Do Women Leave Architecture?", conducted by the Royal Institute of British Architects (RIBA), revealed the extent of the industry's disadvantages. On the study's publication in 2003, the organization's then-president George Ferguson commented: "We have some brilliant women architects but we are losing some of our brightest graduates because of poor working conditions, the macho culture and low pay in the profession. Architectural practice needs to take action if we want to be able attract and keep talented and committed architects in the industry."[41]

The Perception of Female Architectural History

While in the process of researching her biography of Thekla Schild—the second German woman ever to receive a degree in architecture—American architecture professor Despina Stratigakos closely monitored the uploading of a new entry about Schild to Wikipedia. Yet scarcely had the entry been online for thirteen minutes, when a request was made for its speedy deletion. Stratigakos describes the feeling she had as she watched the editorial discussion unfold: "But two things caught my eye (and raised my blood pressure): first, *Der Krommodore* asserted that Schild was not sufficiently accomplished to be listed on Wikipedia; and second, he expressed doubt, that Schild *had ever existed*. During nearly twenty years of writing about women architects, … no one had ever denied the actual existence of my subjects."[42] Whereas Stratigakos was the one who had done the research and verified the information in the entry, *Der Krommodore*, the administrator, alleged that it was a fabrication—because he did not find enough sources to qualify her inclusion in Wikipedia. Stratigakos's anecdote makes clear one of the many snares encountered when trying to make female architectural history visible: anyone who is not googleable today did not exist yesterday. The *impression* arises that the person was not relevant enough. Many women architects of the twentieth century simply cannot stand comparison against the vast body of source information that exists for their male colleagues. In her seminal work *Invisible Women: Exposing Data Bias in a World Designed for Men*, Caroline Criado-Perez elucidates this self-generating systematization, which is brought to bear not only in architectural history: "The presumption that what is male is universal is a direct consequence of the gender data gap. ... But male universality is also a *cause* of the gender data gap: because women aren't seen and aren't remembered, because male data makes up the majority of what we know, what is male *comes* to be seen as universal."[43]

A Question of Relevance

In Wikipedia, the share of female architects among all of the biographies of women amounts to 4.9 percent. In a ranking of thirty professional fields of activity, they occupied third to last place.[44] Only "engineers" and "clerics" have an even lower share of female biographies, although the number of women clerics is so low in part because women may not have been allowed to pursue this profession. How is it possible that women's biographies in the area of architecture remain so far behind?

On Wikipedia's twentieth anniversary, the encyclopedia was criticized for its Western and androcentric perspective. In the context of this lack of diversity, its organizational structure was also the subject of criticism.

While the encyclopedia is compiled entirely by volunteers, only those who write a great deal and regularly contribute to the website can become administrators. With this structure as its basis, the major share of the administrators on German Wikipedia are male, white, and older than fifty. It may be that the gender imbalance in this organizational structure tends to result in a rather coarse, in part discriminatory discussion culture; in the depiction of women, both visually and in texts, from a predominantly male perspective; and in lengthy male and a distinct lack of female biographies. Thus the unfortunate circumstances of female architectural history on Wikipedia encounter a kind of contemporary basis democracy. At first glance, the structure seems equitable but systemic influences are not taken

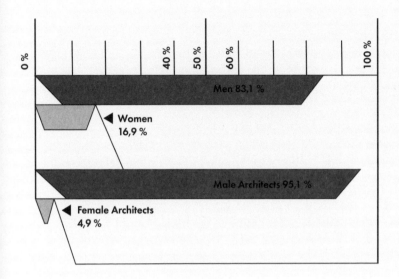

Fig. 4: The share of female biographies in contrast to the
biographies of female architects on Wikipedia Deutschland
Source: Wikipedia Deutschland/Analysis: Karin Hartmann/
Infographic: PAPINESKA

into consideration. However, given that editors must be educated
and with time resources at their disposal, not to mention the total
lack of remuneration, the website is perhaps not as evenly accessible
to the majority of the population as it may seem.

Only that which has relevance gains entry into Wikipedia. Every
professional group has its own set of criteria that make an individual
"relevant" enough to be included in the encyclopedia. The relevance
criteria for biographies in the area of architecture are relatively high:
people are added to Wikipedia if they are represented nationally
among the top one hundred in the BauNetz ranking, have received
notable national or international awards, or if third parties have published about their work. As soon as they become part of an office,
they do not obtain their own lemma in favor of an office website.

If it is already difficult to accommodate contemporary female architects using these relevance criteria, then it becomes even harder in the case of historical personalities. Without pertinent sources, they are not incorporated into the encyclopedia. However, a lack of publications and awards can often be attributed to reasons other than the poor quality of one's architectural oeuvre.

There are several initiatives and alliances whose goal it is to increase the share of female biographies. As part of the international project Women in Red, the initiative Frauen in Rot[45] marks relevant women for whom a biography has not yet been created. In edit-a-thons, groups collaborate on writing a predefined number of women's biographies; in 2015, the initiative WomanD organized temporary edit-a-thons for biographies of women architects.[46] Yet it is quite evident that a major structural step, for example a diversity quota for administrators or a consistent analysis of all relevance criteria with respect to systematically discriminatory admission restrictions, would substantially increase equal opportunity.

A further look at Wikipedia reveals how important sources are in order to make female architectural history visible. Only research into female architects, and the publication of its results, makes it possible to situate them in relation to their male colleagues, who have historically had better working conditions in almost every respect. Not only do more books have to be written, but there is above all a lack of archives that needs redressing. The International Archive of Women in Architecture in Blacksburg, Virginia, is the largest analog archive for handling the estates of women architects from around the world. It contains material from female architects spanning forty different countries and seventeen languages. Besides this, the Dynamic National Archive of Women in American Architecture, of the Beverly Willis Architecture Foundation, comprises the largest online archive for American women architects. In Germany, the Technische Universität Berlin (TU Berlin; Berlin University of Technology) as well as the Deutsches Architekturmuseum (DAM; German Architecture Museum) maintain interesting archival material. As the scholar Mary Pepchinski points out, numerous references to the activities of women may also be preserved in the estates of male colleagues. Inventories are another significant means of revealing this legacy. They contain letters and manuscripts in which relevant material might be found, and thus afford potential researchers the opportunity to examine them.[47] In terms of perspective, a separate online archive comprising, for example, German-speaking countries would also mark an important step toward making female architects and planners better visible and, hence, relevant.

The Legacy and Its Perception

A widespread assumption in the history of architecture is that there were only isolated instances of women architects in the last century, due to admission restrictions and other social hurdles. In 2004, Kerstin Dörhöfer established that the *perception* of the female architectural legacy is more deficient than its reality. In the course of her investigation into women pioneers in architecture, she asked herself whether the contribution made by female architects to building activity was not worth mentioning.[48] She divides twentieth-century women architects into five phases and provides an initial systematic overview of the architectural history of women: "I was not … concerned with the question of whether female architects build differently, which is raised so often (their oeuvre will provide the answer itself) … . For me it was a question of completing the deficient history of women's architecture."[49] How could it happen that, in addition to existing obstacles, the retrospective *perception* of the female architectural legacy has been so severely affected? In order to understand the extent of the repression affecting women architects and their work, it makes sense to call to mind the fact that it wasn't simply one or the other form of discrimination, which are perhaps to be expected in terms of the prevailing culture. Neither was it solely active admission restrictions that limited their work. Rather, it was the overlapping of the effects of *individual, structural,* and *institutional discrimination*[50] that engendered a partial deletion of female architectural history.

Repression

Specific accounts of the works designed by the first German woman architect, Emilie Winkelmann, are rare. There is little mention of her work in books and specialist journals, although her reform architecture was definitely in the same ranks as that of Hermann Muthesius, for example. The active disregard of her oeuvre became apparent during participation in a call for the submittal of designs for the department of oriental languages at the Berlin university: her design ideas found little entry into the sensational coverage of her colleagues Bruno Taut, Peter Behrens, and Hans Poelzig.[51] That didn't only hold true for Winkelmann. As Dörhöfer points out: "Even though Emilie Winkelmann's work was honorably mentioned, hardly any of her drawings were presented or academically discussed, as were the works of many of her male colleagues with comparable architectures. The individual work of specific women architects was not examined more closely and presented."[52] If it was discussed, then it was only with respect to areas that socially pertain to women, such as interiors, the kitchen, décor. Emilie Winkelmann herself made very sober comments about her job: "Practice does not pose any difficulty. How could it even be professionally more difficult for a woman who had the same training as a man."[53] Her critics saw it differently. She was attributed with design qualities for interiors, as was to be expected of a woman. Until recently, Eileen Gray, who with her spectacular home E.1027 designed one of the icons of modernity in 1929, was listed as an interior designer.

The Max-Frisch-Bad, a public swimming pool in Zurich, is an architectural tip for travelers. It is the only structure designed by the writer and architect Max Frisch to have ever been built. The author Ulrike Eichhorn examined the working relationship between him and his wife, Gertrud Frisch-von Meyenburg, during the planning and construction of the outdoor pool. An array of evidence indicates that Trudy Frisch drew a substantial share of the design. Max Frisch's journeys during the crucial phase of the 1943 architectural competition are, for example, well-documented by his diaries. One can also discover Trudy Frisch's characteristic drawing style in the project planning.[54] The couple separated after the pool was built. The outdoor pool became the Max-Frisch-Bad, and according to Wikipedia, "as a public building, it is the only known work of architecture by Max Frisch, and whose design qualities are, from an architectural point of view, considered to be a reference design."[55] The encyclopedia states that Trudy Frisch recommenced her work as an architect after her separation from Frisch.[56] A study of this episode of female architectural history could reveal that as an architect, Max Frisch did not create only one important work, but in fact not a single one.

For women in architecture, institutional admissions restrictions constituted the greatest obstacle for a long time. When they were finally allowed to be admitted to the Weimar Bauhaus, this was reversed. In his inaugural speech in 1919, director Walter Gropius said: "No distinction between fair sex and strong sex. Absolute equality, but absolute equal duties as well. No deference to women; when working, everybody is an artisan."[57] However, this warning apparently did not have the anticipated effect, as women nevertheless showed a real interest in enrolling. As the emancipated image of the "New Woman" developed throughout the 1920s, the reform school drew young women to pursue a course of study. As a result, on the occasion of the 2012 exhibition "Der Architekt: Geschichte und Gegenwart eines Berufsstandes" (The Architect: History and Present of a Profession) in Munich, Ute Maasberg and Regine Prinz established: "An absolute equality of the sexes never occurred [at the Bauhaus in Weimar]. Weaving quickly developed into a pure 'class of women,' albeit without a degree. In most of the other subjects, it was soon made sure that women in general did not gain admittance. Admission into the faculty of architecture was handled restrictively … . Gropius demanded a solid educational background in artisan or practical work. … That made admission virtually impossible for women."[58] In his 1908 book *Die Frau und die Kunst*, Karl Scheffler puts women in their place. They would have to stand clear of architecture.[59] Thus, as Kerstin Dörhöfer sums up, for the Bauhaus in Weimar: "Just as Karl Scheffler, before even a single woman was accepted for

»Mein Ziel ist es, – in diesem Falle! –
von meiner Weiblichkeit abzusehen
und mich ganz selbstvergessen
nur der Bauaufgabe zuzuwenden.«

Prof. Susanne Gross — kister scheithauer gross architekten, Köln

Fig. 5: Statement made by Susanne Gross on
the occasion of the exhibition "Frau Architekt"
in North Rhine-Westphalia in November 2020
Source: Claudia Dreyße

a course of study, had altogether denied the female sex any sense
of space whatsoever, so did it appear that one sought to hinder the
expansion of their professional activity following the first solid evidence to the contrary."[60]
This dates back one hundred years, and is an important piece of
contemporary history. Yet the underlying systematics of institutional
discrimination did not disappear. At the end of the 1990s, private
universities in the United States even began lowering the admission
requirements for young men in order to maintain a gender balance.[61]
Because "too many" women wanted to access a course of study, the

institutions apparently saw the danger of losing their reputation. Professions and entire sectors are lesser valued and lesser paid as soon as they are pursued predominantly by women. It will be interesting to keep an eye on what this fear of femininization means for the professional profile of the architect, which will have to fundamentally shift in order to deal with climate change: a number of female-coded attributes are required to "look after" and "tend to" the existing building stock.

Concern about One's Own Genre

In the field of architecture, fear of femininization and an associated devaluation is deeply internalized. Hence, women architects liked and like to simply refer themselves as "architects", often avoiding the female label. After winning the Pritzker Architecture Prize in 2004, Zaha Hadid said: "I used to not like being called a woman architect: I'm an architect, not just a woman architect."[62] When the exhibition "Frau Architekt" by the Deutsches Architekturmuseum opened in North Rhine-Westphalia in 2020, female architects from the region were sought out to complement historical role models by presenting their own work on a panel. Instead of a work, Susanne Gross submitted the comment: "My aim—in this case!—is to disregard my femaleness and entirely devote myself to the task of building."

The concern that female architectural history behaves in a manner similar to other forms of art is justified: when women appear on the scene, a new genre can develop. The journalist Mareice Kaiser describes this phenomenon with reference to literature: "There are so-called women's books. But there are no men's books. Women's books are for women, men's books are for people."[63] There were many voices in the literature sector that demanded a change—and successfully: today, the literature market, including awards, reviews, and published titles, is far more balanced than it was just a few years ago. The current trend toward feminism contributes to a greater self-confidence and self-image, but concerns about an independent genre based on one's gender continue to exist. At the same time, history shows us that the "norm" has always had one gender: male.

Female Architects as Avantgarde

Before the job title "architect" was protected, the lack of access to training led to numerous self-taught women, some of whom successfully practiced their profession.[64] However, not having received a degree became an argument for taking them less seriously professionally. With the publication of her 2019 biography *Sibyl Moholy-Nagy: Kritikerin der Moderne,* Hilde Heynen brought back to light the work of female architecture critics in German-speaking countries. As the widow of László Moholy-Nagy, she began her career as an architectural historian in the 1950s alongside her activities at the Institute of Design in Chicago. A "travelling observer," she was one of the first to research the quality of North America's regional architecture.[65] Sibyl Moholy-Nagy repeatedly opposed the development of modernity: "In her criticism of the 'stars' of modern architecture—Mies, Gropius, Le Corbusier—she very early on pointed out the untenability of their axioms and the threat of urban vitality ensuing from them."[66] Lining up with her colleagues Jane Jacobs and Ada Louise Huxtable, she criticized the trend toward increasingly functionalistic urban planning as being too little oriented toward human beings. Despite

Fig. 6: Le Corbusier had himself photographed in the nude while painting the murals in E.1027
Source: Fondation Le Corbusier, VG Bild-Kunst Bonn

all her success, as an autodidact she was frequently denied professionality.[67] Although she had published a great deal, had an excellent network, and held a chair at the Pratt Institute, she faded into obscurity after her death. Most of her books are now out of print. Especially in the case of Moholy-Nagy, an examination of the reasons for her reception is interesting from a gender perspective. That she led a free life and chipped away at the image of the "masters" may be why she was particularly sanctioned by the establishment. Sibyl Moholy-Nagy does not yet occupy the place in history that befits her as a multifaceted voice of architectural criticism.

A further injustice in women's architectural history was that collaborative works were often attributed to male colleagues—especially if they were good. Le Corbusier's handling of E.1027, the home built by Eileen Gray in 1929 on the French Atlantic coast, went far beyond that. After she moved out in 1939, Le Corbusier added five large murals to E.1027, published them, and conducted guided tours through Gray's house—in marked contrast to his credo that painting ruined the wall. As a result, he is repeatedly misnamed as the designer of E.1027. Eileen Gray herself was not officially acknowledged as the home's architect until 2000.[68] From today's perspective, this incident can be viewed as a jealous attempt at appropriation that deliberately aimed to erase Gray's authorship. Le Corbusier acted with extreme aggression. Writing in 1939, he claimed he had a "raging desire to sully these walls." "Ten compositions are finished, enough to soil everything."[69] He had himself photographed while painting in the nude, and the paintings contained numerous sexual innuendos.[70] Would his behavior have been conceivable if a male colleague of his had built the house? Eileen Gray is regarded as one of the few women architects of the twentieth century who worked autonomously from the very beginning. She was lesbian, and led a remarkably unconventional and largely self-determined life for her time. Admittedly, she built E.1027 according to Le Corbusier's Five Points of the New Architecture but reinterpreted these in her own terms. Her home wasn't meant to be a machine for living, but an extension of herself.

Following Corbusier's intervention, Eileen Gray never again set foot in E.1027, instead building herself a new home. Corbusier was a world away from this aplomb. He continued to be an obtrusive, jealous presence and built his Cabanon in 1951 on the adjacent lot. Finally, in 1965, he drowned at the foot of the house, on the beach of Cap Martin. Today, Le Corbusier would simply be considered a stalker. Indeed, when Gray attempted to defend herself, he openly threatened to make the fight for the house public.[71]

Le Corbusier seemed to begrudge Gray not only the house itself but, above all, the achievement of her having created it. Outwardly, he could not concede its authorship to her, and apparently not inwardly either. His naked obsession stands in stark contrast with the image of an artistic figure without a private life, as he otherwise stylized himself. Re-evaluating female architectural history also means critically scrutinizing the "masters," who have stood on a pedestal for decades and continue to exercise an influence on the architectural canon.

With Eileen Gray, we see how a similarly autonomous woman was sanctioned many years before Sibyl Moholy-Nagy. At a time when female architects were only successful if they were supported by men, or supported men themselves, she broke character. Numerous "masters" had working or romantic relationships with women architects. Yet were they, on the surface, in a position to have a relationship on a truly equal footing? A large number of works by women were not cited as their individual achievements, but as part of collaborative work.[72] Marion Mahony Griffin, Charlotte Perriand, Lilly Reich, Anne Tyng. History supplies enough examples of these bonds, which in retrospect were rather detrimental to women. In 1974, long after the classic modern era, Denise Scott Brown criticized sexism within the architectural star system.[73] Seventeen years later, the Pritzker Prize was awarded to her equal partner, Robert Venturi, and she was overlooked. When a journalist asked her why she shunned the award ceremony, she criticized a precarious system that relied on male superstars: "You can't make a mom-and-pop-guru," she declared.[74] Today, the distorted perception of female architectural history and the attendant denigration of women's architectural contributions is only intensified by digitalization and artificial intelligence. Just as Google asks, when one enters "*Architektin* [female architect]", "Did you mean *Architekt*?" [male architect]", algorithms also generate a presumably one-dimensional reality. The reality was more likely quite the opposite: in the face of adversity, and sometimes with several children, those women who managed to execute projects and draw an accommodating public *had to* be extremely good. They should be considered avantgarde.

White Men as an Institution

Examining the instruments of repression also means throwing light on the strengthening and solidarity of men among themselves. Sara Ahmed—the British-Australian scholar and pioneer of Critical Race Theory—frames the image of "white men as an institution" that works to bind white male academics together: "Citationality is another form of academic relationality. White men is reproduced as a 'citational relational.' White men cite other white men: it is what they have always done; it is what they will do; what they teach each other to do when they teach each other. They cite how bright he is; what a big theory he has. He's the next such-and-such male philosopher: don't you think; see him think. The relation is often paternal: the father brings up the son who will eventually take his place."[75] Reciprocal citation and mutual referencing, especially in architectural terms, are an immanent part of building history. This could be a further reason why a structural imbalance developed in the first place, and why it continues to manifest in the insufficient perception of the female legacy to this day.

The instruments of repression can be further illustrated based on countless examples. Ultimately, they correspond to the power imbalance of a patriarchal society that is oriented toward a binary understanding of gender, and which places the white, "civilized" citizen at the top of the hierarchy. Everyone else had fewer privileges. In the international discourse, alongside the cry for a more gender-equitable history of architecture, there are an increasing number of calls to reflect on the colonial mindset in architecture.[76]

Reappraisal

In the long term, the reappraisal of the history of architecture can have no lesser goal than a re-canonization in which the erasure of works by women architects from history is identified and reviewed in favor of a new, contemporary, and intersectional approach. Enormous research efforts are required for an architectural history curriculum to be taught in such a way that adequately and meaningfully incorporates factors of gender, class, ethnicity, and race into the discipline's study. Numerous researchers are already working on it, as are initiatives, students, and educators. Professor Kathleen James-Chakraborty was awarded the 2021 European Research Council Grant for her project *Expanding Agency: Women, Race and the Dissemination of Modern Architecture*. Her research aims "to support a more diverse profession that, in the wake of social justice movements such as #MeToo and Black Lives Matter is better prepared to engage with a broad public and address such social challenges as the integration of migrants and sustainability." She adds: "There is thankfully a tidal wave of scholars studying women architects right now but the challenge is to get new scholarship into the classroom and also to demonstrate the other ways in which women and ethnic minorities have contributed to creating the climate for the modern architecture that remains at the core of the curricula of most architecture schools."[77]

It will be interesting to observe how, in particular, the embedding of an intersectional perspective develops in the discipline and how the architectural history yet to be taught will change for the next generation.

In order to achieve this goal, new sources on repressed architectural legacies have to be developed. To address these major gaps, the creation of alternative biographies on Wikipedia could become a part of the course of study. The combination of research and writing, together with the discussion of deletion and preservation, would be an act of political education, as it were, as would the examination of the discriminatory historical narrative. Through becoming Wikipedians, students could embed their newly acquired insights (and insights from subsequent projects) directly in the encyclopedia, thus making interesting source materials available to others. In addition to further research, teaching provides a great opportunity—immediately and at the outset of one's training—to transform the *perception* of the architectural legacy of women and other marginalized groups. Or, as Kerstin Dörhöfer asked in 2004: "When does a tradition begin to evolve that successors can refer to? How does a 'female lineage' take shape? How many generations will it require until a cultural legacy emerges? What accomplishments have to be achieved? And above all: How will that be legacy be passed down?"[78]

Black Turtleneck, Round Glasses

45—55

"Afaina de Jong is not your typical architect."[79]
Afaina de Jong, Studio AFARAI

Based on an analysis of Google News content while conducting *word embedding*, the term *architect* appears in sixth place among the professions most likely to be associated with men, following *maestro*, but still before *warrior* and *fighter pilot*.[80] The job of architect is described as a creative, responsible, and at the same time generalist activity, with positive connotations, almost to the point of being stereotypical. While myth and reality diverge in many places, the positive expectations create a certain positive pressure to live up to them.[81]

From Lone Genius to Star

The image of the profession is characterized by a network of narratives that has grown and evolved over centuries. One of them is the image of the *lone genius*, the solitary author who does everything on his own. The figure is given exaggerated form through the character of Howard Roark in Ayn Rand's book and in the eponymous film *The Fountainhead* (1949), where he is played by Gary Cooper. Rand's close contact with Frank Lloyd Wright suggests that he was the inspiration for the main character. *The Fountainhead* tells the story of an unknown architect who undergoes a metamorphosis from outsider to star. He stubbornly believes in his designs until he is finally able to convince others of his genius. Human relationships are a secondary matter for him. When his version of a design isn't implemented, he ultimately blows up his building. *The Fountainhead* is a plea for individualism. The protagonist Howard Roark typifies a series of doctrines in architecture. Unswerving ambition, complete dedication to the architectural creation, belief in the quality of one's own design against all opposing voices, fame that comes only after a tough ordeal, the merging of the author and his work. He embodies radical creative exertion to the point of addiction, but also the allure that emerges from it, to which everything in his personal life is subordinated.

After the 1991 Pritzker Architecture Prize was awarded to Robert Venturi alone, prompting a debate, the journalist Justin Davidson tersely noted: "But the Scott Brown controversy also shows how hard it is to dismantle the myth of the solitary auteur popularized by Ayn Rand in *The Fountainhead*."[82] Despina Stratigakos likewise refers to the enormous influence that Howard Roark had on students: "Roark, a 'brilliant' architect, is represented as heroically violent, claiming his rights through masculine brutality. ... Roark was, literally, a tough act to follow, and the novel possessed a cultlike status among architectural students for decades after it was published."[83] Howard Roark's contemporary caricature is the architect Rodrigo Tomás, the protagonist of the 2021 novel *The Masterplan*. Rodrigo is offered the opportunity, like an architectural American dream, to build an entire city in Africa. But the dream turns out to be an illusion; in reality, Rodrigo is a puppet of his overpowering father, a postmodern icon.[84] The book's author, Reinier de Graaf, a partner at the Office for Metropolitan Architecture, describes the novel as a "satirical version of my world." He adds: "It's meant to describe the world of international architecture with its upsides and its downsides. ... This is not a confessional diary on my part, although certain experiences I must say come in handy if you have to write the scenes."[85] Tomás's drive to use the prestigious project to obtain the recognition of his father and his colleagues in the *boys' club* takes up the majority of the novel. Women play no role in the satire either.

Walter Gropius and Le Corbusier presented themselves as stars in the 1920s, a practice that only became systematic in the neoliberal 1980s and 1990s. Architects such as Frank O. Gehry, Richard Meier, Rafael Moneo, and Zaha Hadid represent an architecture that was linked with their own name as a brand. The large office structures behind them were only minimally visible to the outside world. Cities such as Herford in Germany "bought" a "Gehry" and marketed both the work and its author.

In 2017 the #MeToo movement arrived in architecture, at least in North America. That was when the *Shitty Architecture Men List* appeared on the Internet—a crowdsourced platform where women and men in architecture could anonymously document sexual misconduct in the profession. The creator of the platform later revealed her motives, explaining: "We're trained to view suffering as deeply related to the work. So something like harassment is easy to dismiss as part of the sacrifice."[86]

Richard Meier temporarily stepped down and, in 2021, retired from his firm after five women had accused him of sexual harassment. The American architecture critic Alexandra Lange subsequently questioned the "classic architect profile" in the star system: "I can now more clearly see [it] as a fiction: that one man (or Zaha) does it all ... . I reckon it is time to put an end to the architect profile as we now know it."[87] Today, roughly one-quarter of the sixty-four firms in the BauNetz ranking operates under the name of a single founder or owner, although alternative forms are on the rise.

There are, of course, the résumés of successful architects that follow a trajectory from penniless beginner to star. In light of these success stories, Mary Pepchinski points out that the intersectional perspective is particularly interesting. "Such stories about women architects are very rare," she says in response to anecdotes about Norman Foster, who worked several odd jobs, including selling ice cream, to finance his university studies. While a number of established architects came from humble backgrounds, the women, up until today, have often had greater financial or non-material support from the outset. One of the few known, historical exceptions is Lotte Stam-Beese.

It is known that she had to work a good deal during her studies. But her family, too, stood behind her.[88]

The star-architect system is part of a masculine tradition, although there are indications that the work itself is coded in a gender-specific manner. Hilde Heynen examined the adjectives used by the Pritzker juries in selecting prizewinners from 1978 onwards, dividing the descriptive terms into those having more female and more male connotation. She also exposed the mentioning of patriarchal lines in the judging of the prize. Sons, fathers, and husbands were mentioned to underscore a positive judgement. Her analysis clustered the masculine- and feminine-coded descriptions and weighted them according to how frequently they occurred. The results revealed that the majority of the works selected tended to be described with masculine-coded terms such as *masterful*, *powerful*, and *heroic*, whereas feminine-identified descriptions like *harmonious* were easily outnumbered. A ratio of 3:1 seemed to be the ideal and most frequently occurring variant. In the case of Zaha Hadid, the ratio was 4:0.[89] Despite all the traditional references, the star-architect system seems to be increasingly losing significance. Forms of multidisciplinary collaboration in diverse teams, such as the British studio Assemble and the Spanish collective Lacol, are now established and formulating new kinds of office culture. Working in a team, on an equal footing, as well as the desire to do so are increasingly part of the self-conception of young women and men who are training as planners.

Insignia and Privileges

The visual description "black turtleneck, round glasses" evokes an image of the "masters" of modernity. Numerous publications attest to the "posturing" of the "traditional architect," identified by visual characteristics, certain gestures, and behaviors derived from the idols of classical modernism.[90] These include minimalistic black clothing, round horn-rimmed glasses, a bowtie, cigar, a shaved head.[91] These visual insignia are not only gender coded; the predominantly black accessories generate the strongest effect when contrasted with a white skin color.

This habitus essentially represents an internalized professional culture that varies depending on the field of study.[92] Inwardly, it provides a feeling of belonging, while outwardly it conveys, for instance, a sense of reassurance to the clients. The impression that a person is closely fused with his profession (and its stereotypes) creates a sense of trust. After all, it's a matter of entrusting him with their unique, large, private or business investments.

This habitus has evolved over time. Today, the fundamentally male-coded markers of the architect's appearance are given additional contrast by, for instance, a colorful accent: maybe sneakers, a hooded sweater, or a ponytail. Along with being female-coded, this soft, sometimes surprising accessory is regarded as a sign of sensitivity and conveys a sense of style. In her Swiss study *Zur Untervertretung von Frauen im Architekturberuf* (On the underrepresentation of women in the architecture profession), the sociologist Christina Schumacher made the following observation: "Through an increased concern for their appearance, male architects draw attention to themselves as such. In the process, they take advantage of a leeway in the representation of professionalism and belonging that is not available to women architects. In contrast to their male colleagues, for women, giving their appearance a particular emphasis is considered gender typical and hence draws attention more to their (wrong) gender than to their professionalism."[93]

The habitus, Schumacher points out, extends far beyond outward features: "Architecture's appropriation of the private sphere takes place via aesthetic, formal factors. 'Good form' … determines the design of one's dwelling, clothing, hairstyle, and accessories as well as how one spends their leisure time. This includes attending opening receptions, exhibitions, and films, dining at 'in' restaurants, as well as traveling to the iconic sites of architecture and urban planning."[94] So far, so good. If everything goes according to plan, the once young, art-loving, and committed architect with round glasses and Moleskine backpack will become a successful silverback. Many architecture firms cultivate an official or unofficial dress code.

The monochromic nature of the profession's image, expressed in reserved clothing and a preference for gray and black, for uniformity rather than diversity, encourages a situation in which personal features and other idiosyncratic markers of one's identity literally fade into homogeneity. The black turtleneck and round glasses are not just markers but also a mask.

Being a Woman Architect and Being a Woman

Even when they have no connection to architecture, many women prefer a simple, pared-down style that emphasizes their personality. This muted aesthetic often represents an incredible reduction of the options that are available to women in terms of clothing, hairstyle, and accessories, as well as an associated "toning-down" of their individual expressions of *joie de vivre* and feminine identity—reductions that women potentially have to contend with for the rest of their lives. Nevertheless, the dress code holds sway. Photos of women architects in the 1980s and 1990s can look like pictures of sisters or cousins. Many perceive the habitus with its dress code as a personal style and not as an abandonment of style's expressive possibilities. In her book *Down Girl*, the social philosopher Kate Manne explores the reciprocal relationship between misogyny and sexism. She explains how misogyny describes the system, defined by stereotypes, in which women are allowed to move in society, while sexism serves to sanction women's behavior when they go beyond that system.[95] Related to the habitus of the architect, this means that the code offered to women often leads them into a role conflict that is difficult to resolve. If they wish to belong, they must abandon those expressive forms ascribed to female persons—and consequently run the risk of being less respected, both as women and within the wider social order. If, on the other hand, they reject the coding offered in favor of their own, uncharted paths, they must forgo certain features of the profession's success and thus its privileges. In terms of the professional culture, Schumacher comes to a similar conclusion: "Many perceive the need to assert themselves in a pointedly masculine world as hardly compatible with their female gender identity. In contrast to their male colleagues, female architects are faced with the task of having to strike a balance between professional and gender identity."[96] This subtle dilemma, which is difficult to grasp, suggests the conflict in which women find themselves in architecture. Another important point is the perspective awaiting women once they become successful. There are indications in the research that competent women are less popular and, in that respect, also pay a high personal price for their career.[97] Dagmar Richter, a professor at Pratt Institute in Brooklyn, outlines in Tanja Kullack's book *Architecture: A Woman's Profession* the impact that a successful career can have on the life of an woman architect: "[W]omen who are respected as authors within the architectural discipline do not have any sort of perspective of personal and psychological benefit. A famous male architect can well work towards a future with several younger wives, lovers, adoring assistants, a well-looked after family in which the woman brings up the children in his interest—without taking up too much of his time—and towards an active, satisfying social, sexual, and love life. ... However, the higher a female architect rises, the more she has to deal with loneliness, social exclusion, childlessness, and hostility and she needs to be aware that personal reward will not materialize. ... Society has not been willing to reward women who have engaged in the profession. Even fewer women have been rewarded for breaking the rules or questioning the status quo. Women are still entirely isolated and socially eliminated if they were willing to take that risk."[98] Not a particularly uplifting prospect. Here, too, positive role models are missing on a broad scale.

A prevalent aspect of the professional culture is also the tendency of women and men architects to seek a partner within the profession. As Christina Schumacher has observed: "Most of the respondents are in a relationship with a partner in the same profession. According to a statistical investigation, this is not a coincidence but in fact a trend in the professional culture."[99] Inés Toscano examined this ongoing dynamic in a survey of 400 architect couples. She notes a pattern of shared biographies: meeting while university students, getting married, sharing an office and family name, participating in competitions, becoming parents, owning a house with an architecture office.

In a seminar at Anhalt University, Toscano conducted a role-playing re-enactment of historical partnerships with her women students. She found that: "With their holistic bodily experience, the future graduates are debunking stereotypical gender roles, making the ghosts in architecture history visible, and dealing with issues in the profession that affect all genders."[100] History has largely ignored *couplings*, as Beatriz Colomina called these productive working relationships in 1999, despite the fact that a considerable number of the "masters" themselves led this sort of private-professional relationship. As a result, architecture's self-perception and habitus can lead to there being a glut of available role models for men, and a total lack for everyone else. The few women who have "made it" in the system are often not recognized as role models by women. They are appreciated professionally, not as exemplars to be emulated. The best example of this is the former "star architect" Zaha Hadid herself. "Where can a woman still be a woman and truly make it in the system or change it? For me, that was the function of a role model," said one of the women interviewed by Rebecca Volpp as part of her investigation of the habitus, *Architektinnen der Zukunft* (Women architects of the future).[101] The good news is that, as a result of examining discrimination in the history of architecture, the representation of many women in the past is now being re-evaluated. Zaha Hadid in particular was subject to several forms of discrimination.[102] Some of the assessments of her and her work were racist and sexist. In conjunction with the 2003 exhibition of her work "Zaha Hadid Architecture" at the Museum für Angewandte Kunst MAK, Vienna's applied art museum, attendants wore T-shirts featuring one of her quotes, "Would they still call me a diva if I were a man?"[103]

Individual Decisions

All in all, for a young woman, admission to the architectural profession could represent a change of direction and—particularly in terms of the issue of motherhood—possibly a definitive change in her personal life plan, or the prospect of fighting against considerable resistance to achieve it. The visual insignia that make us smirk about the "masters" have existential implications for women. To be sure, the promise of belonging by conforming to the habitus also applies to them, just never entirely. And, in those cases where it does, it often comes at an absurdly high price. Architecture as it currently stands, cannot become a true home for women. Even when they sacrifice everything for it—forgo children, and devote thirty years of their life to it—they remain "immigrants" in their own profession. Often, the overarching influences of professional culture and family policy are individualized. Legally, women have all the options, and are able to make new and different choices. The reality *is* diverse, and biographies remain individual in the details. But individualizing decisions leaves out systemic influences. As the journalist Mareice Kaiser put it: "Breaking free from societal expectations is not an individual decision. They are there, we all feel them, they have an impact on us. We are only free when the alternative of our decisions seems livable, without being branded from the outside."[104] Her statement corresponds to Kate Manne's findings: for fear of possibly being subject to social sanctioning, women often tend to adjust their behavior.[105]

Cultural Change in Sight

The strongly male-codified habitus is expressed in the gaining of privileges—and power. In most cases, the intention is not so much to actively exclude women, but rather to acquire and maintain privileges for themselves. Particularly, the advantages that are achieved mostly unconsciously through the habitus are not necessarily recognized and appreciated as such. Yet they are ultimately—as in other systems of discrimination—enjoyed, used, and seen as a given: one feels comfortable, it just fits. And the highly competitive field of architecture is greatly coveted. The high stakes take their toll. Yet it is unacceptable that women pay an even higher price of admission. Parity means, in the long run, that one side must relinquish power. Observations from the workplace—and this also reflects social developments—show that the commitment to gender justice starts to lag when one's own job is at stake.

Any cultural change needs to ensure that women remain themselves, and what's more, that their capabilities and experiences are allowed to change the system. Adopting masculine attributes is counterproductive for women as long as society continues to expect the opposite from them.

For men, gendered attributes such as physical looks or appearance are in no way a hindrance in the architectural profession; on the contrary, they have been tailormade for them. Many aspects of their personality and masculinity lead them closer to the professional culture, provided that they don't want to set any divergent priorities. How much leeway does the architect's corset allow for a modern, fulfilling fatherhood, one in which men split the care work with their female partner 50:50? Indeed, young fathers wishing to spend a good deal of time with their children might encounter more resistance than mothers and be reminded of their role under the sway of narratives lived out in office culture. As part of its investigation into the *maternal wall bias*, the AIA study came to the following conclusion in its evaluation of the caring father: "Fathers who play an active role in family care are less likely to be promoted or get raises, and are more likely to be pushed out of the workplace. This flexibility stigma is actually a femininity stigma: Fathers who care for their children are seen as less masculine and get penalized for it in the workplace."[106]

A cultural change in planning should be institutionally anchored and supported by everyone and must stem from the very center of professional discourse. It is a major professional-culture feat that must be tackled by all. That is why it is necessary for men to also share in the responsibility and help to shape the change toward realizing a professional culture that meets women's actual needs. And that above all *remains open* to different ways of working and living. Women would do well for themselves by not bending or denying their personality and identity in order to comply with a professional culture that continues to cling to clearly obsolete role models. They would be doing the only sensible thing: turning their attention to other exciting prospects that are more welcoming to them.

The AIA study presents important indications about the imbalance in the industry. The industry's typical attitude toward racism and sexism goes far beyond a mere recognition of the problem.[107] Cathleen McGuigan, editor-in-chief of the American magazine *Architectural Record,* commented on the findings of the study into sexism and racism in her editorial in January 2022, saying: "Among the few positive observations in this damning document: 'Racism and sexism in the profession were so open that we found a pattern of white men noting it with distaste, something we found in no other industry.' It is those white men who have the power to bring about real change to the inequitable workplace they have perpetuated. Gentlemen, if you're disgusted, please do something about it—and then do more."[108]

Learning Architecture

*"I had a terrific professor my first semester: Clotilde Barto.
The first thing she said to us was: I prohibit you from looking
at architecture magazines. You have to go to the theater, read
books, get to know each other, and you'll see that all of these
things will come together."*[109]
Océane Vé-Réveillac, fem_arc collective

In 1926, Ernst Neufert began to "systematically gather lessons learned
from heterogeneous practice and teaching activity" and to compile
them in his *Bauentwurfslehre* (Architects' Data). The 600-page book
serves as a crucial reference for designers and is a standard gift given to students when they begin studying architecture.[110] The forty-
second edition still contains his "prolegomena," in which he divulges
the secrets of the profession: "Once one has discovered trust in
oneself, insight into relationships, the play of forces, the materials,
the colors, the dimensions; whoever can internalize reality, the appearance of structures, study their impact, critically reflect on them,
reconstruct them in their mind, is on the only true path towards
the great enjoyment of life that only the actively creative individual
feels. This outlook on life should help to take him there."[111] The
"prolegomena" reads like a fantastic future promise, a promise to

one day be allowed to join the ranks of the "elders." The precondition is that the student becomes completely involved, is not deterred by any doctrine, and takes a stand against all traditions. The only thing that counts is one's own will to design: "A born architect ... is so full of his own ideas and ideals that he only needs the elements in order to go the extra mile ... ."[112]

Initiation Rituals

Many of Neufert's premises of successful work have become part of the professional culture and continue to have an effect alongside more recent role models. They become apparent in particular in departments that attract students by means of particularly rigorous teaching and thus implicitly promise training for "genuine, uncompromising designing." Students are intended to become "obedient architecture soldiers"; alongside initiation rituals, the "fifth night shift" and harsh criticism help to train the real architecture personality.[113] The "school of hard knocks" is not a generational issue. Among younger professors it can also be observed that this framing is helpful to obtain a chair and lead it successfully. A male professor in a German department of architecture describes how the male-coded attitude influences teaching and how radical, strongly concept-driven architectures that are strictly and rigorously enforced live on as a specific notion of good architecture. Yet not only do these initiation rituals confer the title of architect, and symbolize admission into the profession, they also outwardly exclude people. This is felt especially by those who have not studied architecture but want to contribute something to the discourse: "Those who have landed in this professional field by a circuitous route often quickly realize that they are tolerated at most. At universities, teachers ... assume the responsibility of the gatekeeper," observes the architect and scholar Torsten Lange. The signs of this closure also include a shared canon that constitutes the "allegedly mutual basis for discussion", yet remains unnamed with respect to its powerful construction.[114] In her Swiss study, Christina Schumacher established that students already practice this demeanor during their training.[115] They also

learn what constitutes the professional culture, which later continues in practice: working under high pressure and with an utter commitment to architecture that puts content above their own needs.
They learn to work for nothing for a fulfilling job. Why architects
themselves endorse performing one to two work phases of the German HOAI (Schedule of Services and Fees for Architects and Engineers) for no charge in open competitions remains a phenomenon
for other professional groups. With its ritualized entrenchment in
training, this practice is hardly reflected on after one has graduated.
The other image implicitly transported by Neufert—that the architect is the only one self-sufficient enough to put things to paper—not
only excludes outside criticism but erodes context as well. Resistance to outside influences proves to be especially counterproductive
for integrative design approaches of any kind and tends to correspond with a colonial mindset. There can be no architecture without
users or buildings without context.

Very many of today's practicing architects are familiar with this form
of teaching. Among architects, the special framework conditions are
condoned by claiming that the "laboratory situation" at university is
the only place where one is given free rein to design. This implication
overlooks the fact that this freedom is bought through the practice of
self-exploiting work behavior and maintaining an exclusive attitude.

Learning through Imitation

Architecture departments essentially define themselves by way
of their chairs of design. The chair serves as a poster child for the
department and provides an indication of the practicing school. The
Swiss study analyzes how, in design departments, knowledge is not
communicated through theory, which students can acquire from
textbooks, but through the practical knowledge of experience.[116]
Experiences are passed on firsthand by way of "tabletop criticism"
or "defense." As Christina Schumacher points out, the transfer of
knowledge is more likely than usual to be linked with persons of
influence. The designing of working space, learning methods and
techniques, supplemented by personal criticism, take place through

imitation. "The academic teachers, professors of architecture, as well as national and international stars on the architecture scene are the physical role models for students." Knowledge embodied in this way can thus hardly be separated from the person or from their gender: "For young men, the depicted mimetic learning as a kind of master-pupil learning relationship is much easier, more obvious, and more self-evident than for young women."[117] The foundation for forms of patrilineal expansion is laid out in this teaching practice.

In a 2017 survey of women's representatives focusing on the situation of female architecture students at the Technical University of Munich, students reported having experienced discrimination, for example during presentations, "where they did not feel they were being taken seriously."[118] In Great Britain, a 2014 study by the *Architects' Journal* revealed that "a 'shocking' 54 percent of the female students responding to an international survey on the status of women in architecture claimed to have experienced sexual discrimination in university."[119] In a survey conducted in 2020 of 400 students in the department of architecture at the Technical University of Vienna, 42 percent of those questioned reported having been victims of discrimination.[120] There is currently no data in Germany on discrimination against female students—whether Black, white, or of color—and other marginalized groups during architectural training. However, there are indications that it exists. In order to be able to assess, analyze, and change the structures in teaching, it is urgently necessary to look into data on this and listen to those who have been impacted by discrimination.

Change in Teaching
During the second wave of feminism in the United States, an independent school, the Women's School of Planning and Architecture, was founded between 1975 and 1985. During the summer months, seven women offered experimental course content, free of stereotypes, as part of a summer school.[121] Part of the teaching method was an eye-level approach between teachers and students with the aim of minimizing the role of the teacher as an authority.

As early as forty years ago, women addressed issues of authority and equality in architecture. This approach is also reflected in the interviews with numerous female professors conducted by Tanja Kullack. Many of them emphasize that they place no value on allowing themselves to be "idolized," and instead teach students to work a great deal in teams and to evaluate their performance as the product of a group effort.[122] Hence, they teach in a less individualistic way, concentrating instead on the course material and not on the "affected behavior" of the educational habitus. Many male professors likewise reject male-coded styles of teaching and turn toward more open-ended formats and teaching practices.

A great deal indicates that an increased share of female professors, in particular, will alter the teaching perspective. The number of female professors and visiting professors in architecture departments has risen in recent years.

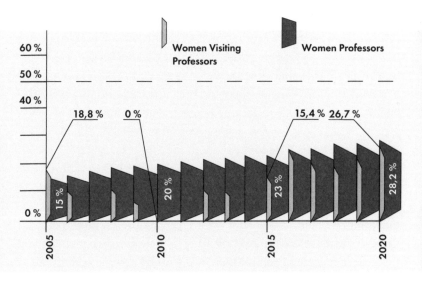

Fig. 7: Women professors and visiting professors in architecture in Germany in 2005–20
Source: Federal Statistical Office of Germany/Analysis: Karin Hartmann/Infographic: PAPINESKA

In addition to appointing new chairs, new content is also finding its way into teaching. One example worth mentioning here is the series of lectures by thirty-six international women architects that was organized by Ursula Schwitalla at the University of Tübingen. The successful format resulted in the publication *Women in Architecture: Past, Present, and Future.*[123] The seminar Gender Masquerade (introduced in the chapter "Black Turtleneck, Round Glasses"), which was led by Inés Toscano, examined the issue holistically and allowed female students to physically experience different gender positions by means of role play. As a visiting professor of the collective Claiming*Spaces, Afaina de Jong taught architecture as an intersectional-feminist practice, in her Space of Freedom at the Technical University of Vienna. In the architecture department of the Technical University of Munich, every semester two lectureships are assigned by women's representatives.

The architect Ingalill Wahlroos-Ritter, interviewed by Tanja Kullack, considers the position of women, in particular outside of the classic architecture career, as a special opportunity for change: "Exciting possibilities in architecture emerge when people don't follow the conventional path of practicing architecture through licensure. I think that women are more likely to find it perfectly acceptable not to become licensed, as many don't see that as a very satisfying way of working. We should encourage our students to consider alternative ways of practicing architecture. It is no accident that women are leading the way in reconsidering praxis."[124]

Calling without Theory

Analogous to communicating practical knowledge, design professors are not appointed via the usual qualification process such as dissertation and habilitation, but from practice.[125] More informal and less quantifiable criteria can lead to men receiving preferential treatment. In order to change this, measures are required that go beyond the goal of a coequal composition of the appointments committee. Changing this procedure means improving the process and the criteria until they work. According to what criteria are women shortlisted during a test run? What formal, transparent, and quantifiable selection criteria can be used? Do these selection criteria have a gender bias? Are they equally satisfiable by all groups of people? Are the criteria more likely to be satisfied by men? What role does self-branding play, for example? This also includes examining the grounds for rejecting a professorship. What basic conditions would a woman have wanted in order for her to accept a professorship?

The filling of design professorships from practice also implies that there is less resonance between teaching and, for example, architectural science. The architect and professor of interior design Carola Ebert compared seminars on architectural education and determined that these strongly orient themselves toward current tendencies in professional practice in terms of both subject and content. As such, they are less oriented toward science, and incorporate few impulses from scientific discipline and subject didactics. "Complex issues, such as the adaptation of curricula to a changing professional job description or the necessary comparison with what women architects require for professional practice, can be just as little answered by drawing on a mixture of individual experience, values, ideals, traditions, and requirements from the reality of university policy, and the profession of architect, as it can by drawing on history alone." She sums up that inquiries into what students expect from and experience during their studies, and into their onward journey through life, would make their perspective in the discourse around architectural teaching much more visible: "Instead of programmatically discussing and framing new goals, in this way the actual impact of architectural teaching could be analyzed and compared with educational objectives."[126] Her analysis reveals how much subject-didactic knowledge does not reach architectural theory, and it also provides an explanation for the fact that the "mimetic master-pupil learning" described by Schumacher is still practiced in the twenty-first century as well. This might also be an explanation for the fact that subject-related content often does not, or only in the case of special interest, reach the faculty.

When, in 2021, a female student wanted to choose the topic of gender-specific use of public spaces at a German university as the subject for her bachelor thesis, she initially received no major support. The first thing the assistants did was to call into question the relevance of her subject. Finally, they recommended literature related to art instead of urban development, and her male professor—a well-known architectural theorist—advised her to look for subject-related articles in the women magazine *EMMA*. After all, this was a new, largely uncharted field. It was the student herself who brought the state of research and relevant sources to the chair, after having examined the extensive literature and used it to support her thesis.[127] One wants to laugh and cry at the same time, since what's worse than the total ignorance of scores literature from over forty years' research on the connection between, gender, architecture, and space, at the epicenter of Germany's architectural education system. The cry for diverse, gender-specific research that will account for inequality in architecture and planning is justified—yet it also requires the will to implement the results and, prior to that, to become aware of them in the first place. Most German architecture departments remain largely unchecked by the demands of feminist theory for more gender-equitable planning. Concentrating on their self-referential discourse, the teaching doesn't cover important subjects that do not stem directly from practice, such as, for example, the enormous relevance of built environment education. Despina Stratigakos also establishes this for the North American discourse: "Today these many decades of research and publications amount to a substantial and significant body of literature on women and gender in architecture. Yet its impact remains limited, because the knowledge and insights it offers rarely find their way into the curricula of architecture schools … ."[128] For Germany, Carola Ebert concludes that architectural teaching's engagement with fields such as university didactics or educational research would be desirable.[129]

All in all, awareness of research in the sector seems to have grown. In the meantime, numerous offices continue to undertake research projects in parallel with their building activities. However, in this context it is often a question of applied research. Initiatives such as the Netzwerk Architekturwissenschaft, at the Technical University of

Munich, are a good example of how teaching, practice, and research are combined and how the transfer of knowledge can be furthered. Annual themes, such as Figurations of Gender in 2020/21, can also contribute to reducing knowledge gaps and exchanging research findings.

On the whole, and in particular due to the accumulation and overlapping of various factors, such as the approach to design, an androcentric history of building, and a lack of role models, exclusionary messages are also communicated in teaching. Christina Schumacher sums it up as follows: "As a result, for young women tendencies towards exclusion are already laid out in the context of education. Even before they enter the professional field, on a symbolic level they are equipped with inferior tools and have less self-confidence, something that for young men grows out of the sense of being in the right place in this profession."[130]

The greatest opportunities for change lie in teaching. It is precisely its practical connection with what is often informally-framed teaching content that makes it possible to embrace relevant, gender-specific content—in this context, it is the responsibility of teachers and chairs to determine which subjects are put on the agenda. In terms of perspective, a shift in the concept of the profession and an increasing number of women in teaching positions, might lead to different teaching practices and to different content.

Do Women Design Differently?

"There is nobody against this [plan]—
NOBODY, NOBODY, NOBODY,
but a bunch of, a bunch of MOTHERS!"[131]
Robert Moses, cited by Jane Jacobs

The question most frequently asked at panel discussions on equal opportunity in architecture is: do women actually design differently than men? Is there such a thing as feminine architecture? Whatever the answer, further questions are certain to follow.

If the answer is in the negative, the question of justifying the effort arises. If the work is of a high quality anyway, what does it matter who designs and builds it? Is it worth changing the structures of a traditional industry to that end?

If the question is answered in the affirmative, there is a concern about reinforcing gender stereotypes. Won't the knowledge that women design better kindergartens possibly lead to their being limited to these and similar tasks?

Questions and answers imply that a "norm" exists, a status quo that might be infringed upon by new, different content or forms of designing. After all, what does it mean to design *differently*? Different from whom or what?

Achieving equal opportunity in architecture means providing equal accessibility to the labor market and leadership positions for all, given equal qualifications. Both hypothetical answers omit the fact that the causes for a lack of equality lie in the discrimination that is common in the industry and completely ignore the perspective of those subject to discrimination. Particularly the recourse to the quality debate falls short; after all, what is meant by quality? And for whom?

A smart woman at the Women in Architecture festival in Berlin in 2021 responded to the question by saying: *people* design differently, because *people* live differently, and each contributes their particular outlook on life to the design. People who work the whole year at home incorporate this perspective when designing residential buildings. People who have to do things in several places in the city develop different mobility concepts than commuters. The assumption that planners can think their way into every possible situation of life is an overestimation and, at the same time, an overload. This is why mixed teams from all areas of experience also achieve the best performance in architecture.

The Poelzig Family Home Office

How the realities of one's own life can be given expression in design is visible in the floor plan of the house designed by Marlene Poelzig in Berlin. In 1930 the architect designed a spacious residential house with architecture office in Berlin's Westend district, near Grunewald, for herself and her family, which comprised three children and several servants. The garden was largely designed in collaboration with the garden architect Herta Hammerbacher.[132]

The concept of the house has several special features. With a large, glazed surface, the *Großes Atelier* (large studio) faces the front garden, garage, and street. The outdoor spaces bordering the Grunewald are zoned according to various recreational uses, including a *Rasenspielplatz* (lawn play area), a *Kinderspielplatz* (children's playground), and *Wasserbecken* (small swimming pool). Adjacent to the kitchen and dining room is the *Kinderspielzimmer* (children's playroom), which opens toward the garden with a swimming area for children. All of the private spaces are oriented toward the Grunewald, except for one: the *Kleines Atelier* (small studio), Marlene

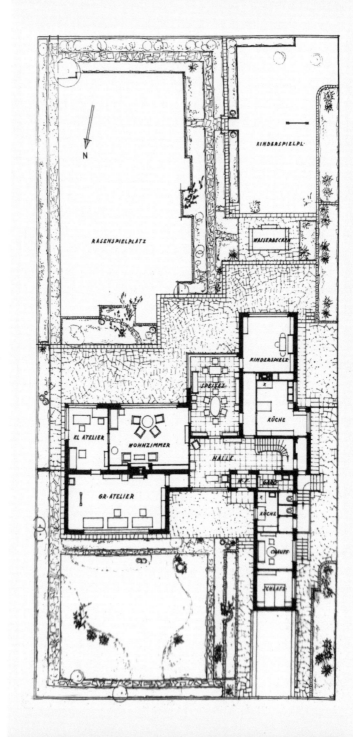

Fig. 8: Floor plan of the house designed by Marlene Poelzig, Berlin-Westend

Source: Scan from *Bauwelt* 1930, no. 34

Poelzig's workspace. From here she could keep an eye on the overall situation. She could see all the outdoor spaces that were accessible to the children and also, through the staggered façade, when someone entered the house. For, even if a nanny and chauffeur lived in the house as well, that wouldn't have relieved Poelzig of responsibility for managing the family's various goings on.

One special feature of the design is that the children's playrooms are located on the same level as the living room and work areas. In contrast to the *Großes Atelier*, Marlene Poelzig's room had access to the living room. Poelzig probably liked having her children nearby and just as likely used every opportunity to be able to work. Short distances in the house, along with generally keeping the children occupied with various play and water areas, may have allowed her to perform her job in a more fulfilling manner. Working parents with small children know how important it can be to use off-peak hours in their daily lives, while still being accessible to them.

The floor plan of the house indicates who was responsible for the care work and its organization. The couple sat—seen from the floor plan—back-to-back. Hans Poelzig was able to receive guests and coordinate his employees undisturbed in his *Großes Atelier*. From there, he could gaze into the front garden without worrying about his children—while others were in charge of keeping them busy and raising them on the back side of the house.

Care

The absence of *care*[133] often forms the crux of the debate on the gender equitable city and contemporary residential dwellings, as well as questions about the gaps that emerge in the built environment when only one population group is responsible for planning them.[134] At the same time, the low value placed on *care* as a part of life, as well as in the professional profile and its narratives, represents something of a flash point in the question of why women leave architecture.[135] For women, motherhood, the epitome of *care* work—or even the desire for it—is probably just an occasion to temporarily turn their backs on architecture in the course of their lives. *Care* tasks relegated women to the suburbs; *care* has rarely been foregrounded as a central task in the history of the city. Today, this deficit is being increasingly noticed and criticized in the social debate. *Care* is relevant at any scale of planning. Regardless of who is performing the care work—an environment geared toward it, from housing and the neighborhood to the city, helps to get it done.[136] *Care* forms the basis of every society and every economy—worldwide. Humans cannot survive without care work. *Care* is work for life. *Care* is economy.[137]

In her essay "Architecture and Care," Elke Krasny demonstrates that the idea of the modern architect has been decisively influenced by the construction of binary oppositions in traditional Western thinking. Binary oppositions establish a relationship in which one side is privileged and the other devalued, such as through feminization and *othering*.[138] Referring to three canonical instances in architecture history—antiquity, the Renaissance, and the Enlightenment—Krasny reveals how, initially, the separation of nature and culture allowed the sheltering aspect of architecture to be split off and assigned to nature. As a result, Krasny explains, architecture acquired the essential trait of not taking the surrounding environment as its starting point. "Modern architecture," she writes, "is very often built on the tabula rasa claim, a deeply colonial mechanism that annihilates nature and everyone and everything that existed on and with the land before."[139] She goes on to say that feminist theory across disciplines has long pointed out that this separation is not right and makes people incapable of responding in a caring and consistent manner to today's trauma of climate change. In light of this crisis, Krasny describes how urgent it is to dissolve this binary opposition: "Care is needed for survival of an exhausted planet with its rate of catastrophes indicating that it is about to reach its breaking point. ... The need for architecture as care is more urgent, and more obvious, than ever."[140]

At the same time, her essay makes it clear how deeply ingrained the binary opposition is in the professional profile of architect, because even once women were admitted to the profession, little changed in this regard: "The field of architecture ... has managed to absorb and incorporate women practitioners without moving toward an ethics of care."[141] Looking at its genesis, one almost gets the impression that the self-conception of the profession is based on this split-off. Even so, *care* has to be understood as more than just reproductive work. The care-related issues of production, protection, and financial responsibility are, as Joan C. Tronto points out, mainly attributed to men: "So when men work and bring home a paycheck, they describe this activity as a form of care."[142] Linda Scott describes how the financial impact changes when women assume financial responsibility. Greater equality and improving women's access to the job market lead to a higher gross domestic product (GDP). According to studies in 163 countries, this applies not only to the third world but also industrial nations. In doing so, women are not taking existing jobs but instead create additional jobs. The decisive factor for economic growth is the use of their income: "[W]omen, as a group, spend [their money] first on their families, especially children, and communities."[143] Women's investment in the community thus contributes to stabilizing the middle class, which is required for a stable market economy.[144] This data sheds new light on the German debate surrounding the financing of good and comprehensive childcare. Improving women's access to the job market is a well-known growth opportunity in Germany.

The architect and earthen architecture expert Anna Heringer also takes the use of building costs into account in every project. During the construction of the METI school in Bangladesh, she attached great importance to ensuring that the costs of her buildings benefitted the community. By employing dug-up mud, a local material that laypeople themselves could prepare on site, the wages went directly back to the local community: "The building budget did not only have a school as a result, but it was also a catalyst for local development. ... Architecture is dealing with a lot of money and yes we can contribute to social justice."[145]

Designing without Context

The low value placed on the environment and context as part of the design approach reflects a colonial mindset that correlates with the figure of the "explorer" who seeks, finds, appropriates, designs, and determines how people are supposed to live. Leslie Kern describes this fundamental attitude found both in geography and in planning: "The masculine, colonial tropes of intrepid explorers mapping the 'new world' still ripple through the field of geography. Urban geographers seek out the next interesting neighborhood to study and social group to classify, while planners aspire to heights of technical, rational, and objective decision-making about how people should live in cities."[146]

The attitude of valuing the existing context less than a new design has become part of the professional culture and, to a large extent, how teaching is understood. It is likewise seen in representations of architecture with as few traces of user paraphernalia as possible and flares up in discussions when award-winning architecture, once in operation, is "not understood" by users. It manifests the separation of user quality from design, which remains independent and, as an autonomous work in itself, can be determined as "good" or not regardless of its functionality. Changing this attitude is a major challenge. But that is precisely what is being questioned in order to bring about a change in the professional profile, and there are many women and men architects who are active in this area. Architecture by Lacaton & Vassal broke with this tradition and created new ways of seeing. In the process of renovating the high-rise slab Le Grand Parc in Bordeaux, for instance, they made the individual furnishings of 530 apartments part of their architecture, thus focusing on the quality and perspective of use.

Criticism of the City Now

A look at the built cities in existence today makes it clear which perspectives are missing in planning. They expose the blank spots left by marginalized groups and women as a result of not being actively engaged, because their voices were not heard, or they didn't occupy a decision-making position. Now, the question of whether today's cities do justice to the needs of *all* population groups is finally being confronted in society. Voices of care providers express doubts about the quality of the status quo and draw attention to poor planning on both large and small scales. Among the frequently cited deficiencies in the planning of public spaces are public toilets, barrier-free access, a lack of seating areas, neglecting multimodal paths, and prioritizing automobile traffic.[147]

If *care* was better integrated as a normal component of our architecture, and more attention was devoted to city planning, adults would be less exhausted. Couples could more easily share their workload and would have more time for their jobs, their children, and themselves. In *Feminist City*, Leslie Kern explains how instead we live in cities that fatigue care workers by consistently failing to meet their needs: "The constant back and forth of day care, school, errands, lessons, visits to family and friends. I want to go back in time and tell myself: stay home. Lie down. Do less."[148] Instead of providing a good way of satisfying care work as part of the everyday surroundings in the built environment, the neoliberalism of the 1990s, Kern points out, led to a worsening of the situation and an aggravation of disparities: "Under neoliberalism, most of the 'solutions' generated for those problems [addressing care] have been market-based, meaning they require the ability to pay for extra services, conveniences and someone else's underpaid labor. Very few changes ... have re-imagined and re-worked the built environment ... in ways that take care work seriously."[149] But, with the exception of special projects such as the Seestadt Aspern in Vienna, cities are rarely planned in a few years and in one piece. As a result, our cities will remain visible for a while longer as Jane Darke vividly described them: "patriarchy written in stone, brick, glass and concrete."[150]

Jane Jacobs and Robert Moses

In 1933 the Athens Charter proclaimed a "functional city," a trend-setting decision that had a worldwide impact well into the postwar period. This nascent urban landscape was criticized by a number of women, most prominently, however, by Jane Jacobs. A resident of Greenwich Village in Manhattan, she loved her vibrant neighborhood and closely followed the urban development of large-scale settlement projects. When the influential head planner Robert Moses planned an express highway through Manhattan in the 1950s as part of a car-centered planning project, Jacobs mobilized a neighborhood protest. In 1961 the journalist published her book *The Death and Life of Great American Cities*, in which she described her observations and proposed solutions for the urban quality of the large city. According to her analysis, this is achieved in dense, mixed-use neighborhoods. The many different viewpoints directed at the streets contribute to a large mutual dependability and hence the neighborhood's safety. Meanwhile, urban policy, led by Robert Moses, sought to replace the dense neighborhoods perceived as "slums" with a large-scale housing policy.[151] The battle dragged on for several years. Jacobs was able to unite many influential voices against the Lower Manhattan Expressway. In a hearing of the townspeople, the only time Jacobs and Moses came face-to-face, Moses lost his composure, claiming: "There is nobody against this—NOBODY, NOBODY, NOBODY, but a bunch of, a bunch of MOTHERS!"

The plan was ultimately dismissed. The expressway would have severely cut up many of the neighborhoods that make Manhattan so appealing today. Attractive, centrally located spaces such as Washington Square Park would have had to make way for a freeway onramp. The years-long confrontation between Jacobs and Moses has subsequently become part of Manhattan's collective memory.[152] The collaborative work *A Marvelous Order* offers a take on the struggle in the form of an opera that will premiere in 2022.[153]

Jacobs's criticism was largely ignited by the attitude of those responsible for making decisions on the drawing board about how people should live.[154] She called for planning decisions to be oriented toward people and context. From today's perspective, the conflict reflects in exemplary fashion the different attitudes of a top-down politics and bottom-up approaches, as well as a clash of planning on different scales. Whereas the leading figures of the Athens Charter were utopians, Jane Jacobs started from her immediate situation, right outside her door. Some sixty years after the battle in Manhattan, Leslie Kern criticizes an overly theoretical approach to planning: "Planning considers itself an objective, rational, and scientific field of study and practice. It's oriented ... to providing services to a faceless imagined 'citizen.'"[155]

Today, very popular cities such as Copenhagen, Paris, Barcelona, and New York have initiated substantial restructuring processes to increase their attractiveness. Even though these developments are the result of teamwork rather than a single individual, they were largely initiated, managed, or overseen by women. Copenhagen was given shape by its city architect Tina Saaby between 2010 and 2019. In resonance with Denmark's approach to architectural policy, she implemented architecture and urban development in Copenhagen on a human scale.[156] Since 2014 Paris has considerably changed its urban quality thanks to the creative drive of its mayor, Anne Hidalgo.[157] Barcelona's mayor, Ada Colau, won the local elections in 2015 not as a member of party but as a candidate of the civic platform Barcelona en Comú. Her agenda includes participatory processes at eye level as well as a less touristy, more livable city.

New York

In New York, during Janette Sadik-Khan's term in office as transportation commissioner between 2007 and 2013, large sections of Broadway as well as Times Square and Herald Square were finally rededicated and redesigned for pedestrians, cyclists, and bus traffic. She thus realized one of Manhattan's most spectacular and radical transformative redesigns.[158] In conjunction with the publication of her book *Street Fight: Handbook for an Urban Revolution*, in which she describes the obstacles she had to overcome for the restructuring, her former supervisor Michael Bloomberg commented: "Janette Sadik-Khan is like the child that Robert Moses and Jane Jacobs never had: an urban visionary determined to reshape the streets of New York."[159] Long before Sadik-Khan launched the improvement of urban spaces, Liz Christy laid the cornerstone in the early 1970s for urban gardening in New York. As an artist, she had observed the neglect in her neighborhood, Alphabet City in the Lower East Side, and founded the Green Guerillas. In 1973 the interdisciplinary community garden group began tossing Christmas-tree-ornament-sized "seed grenades" into abandoned lots "to start a literal grassroots revolution."[160] A year later, the city leased the group a space for a token fee of dollar a month. Liz Christy's garden was the first community garden approved by the city. In 1978 the idea was consolidated in the agency GreenThumb, which was set up to support community-managed gardens. Today over 500 community gardens contribute to New York's climate resilience.[161]

Barcelona

Barcelona has a relatively long tradition of gender-sensitive planning. Since 2005, the Col·lectiu Punt 6 in Barcelona—a cooperative whose members come from the fields of architecture, sociology, and city planning—has taught, studied, and designed strategies and concepts for a city with greater gender equity. The *Urbanismo Feminista* (urban feminism) formulated also by the cooperative is based on a model that addresses all city dwellers equally and makes collective care-taking the starting point of all city-related decisions.[162] The Spanish wordplay consisting of *ciudad* (= city) and *cuidar* (= to care) is combined into *La Ciudad Cuidadora*, the Caring City. Women architects such as Tatiana Bilbao have adopted, among other things, this notion as the departure point for the development of the "house of care," which benefits all relationships by making shared care possible.[163] During the Covid-19 pandemic, the Barcelona Laboratory for Urban Environmental Justice in collaboration with Col·lectiu Punt 6 conducted a study about how public spaces increased health and wellbeing for citizens.[164] For *La Ciudad Amable*, or the Friendly City, a civic participatory project initiated by women to increase the quality of living in Seville, the illustrator María del Mar Muriel developed a graphic that represents *La Ciudad Cuidadora*.[165]

Vienna

Vienna is known for its high quality of life. At the same time, it is Europe's model city in terms of *gender planning*.[166] This is largely due to the commitment of the city planner and feminist urban planning expert Eva Kail. Since the 1990s she has overseen the implementation of gender-sensitive planning in the City of Vienna. Kail's aim is to ensure that an equity policy is also reflected in the urban landscape.[167] Not only have many gender-inclusive spaces been realized during her long tenure. But, perhaps most significantly, strategies were developed and solidified for making *gender planning* an integral part of all municipal planning processes, based around the principle of the *Stadt der kurzen Wege* (City of short distances). Since projects, once realized, are tracked according to their intended use, over thirty years of practical experience have created a deep base of knowledge.[168] This can be seen in the city itself: open spaces like the Reumannplatz—also called Reumädchenplatz (*Mädchen* = girl) by the city's residents because of its spaces designed by, and for, girls—and the Bruno-Kreisky-Park make it possible to experience how quality gender-inclusivity looks and functions in practice. The Seestadt Aspern, a new place to live and work in the east of Vienna, was built taking a gendered perspective into account from the outset. The streets were primarily named after women, which was rarely the case earlier in the city's history. The founder of Vienna's Frauen*Spaziergänge (Women's Walks), Petra Unger, refers to the impact this has: "Every street that is named after a woman is an investment in the city's collective memory."[169] Moreover, a network of different actors has emerged in Vienna, devoted to exploring the subject of gender and space in the broadest sense.

Influences from Europe and around the World

At the European level, *gender mainstreaming* was formalized as a binding political strategy for every form of public *governance* in 1999 as a result of the Treaty of Amsterdam. The concept refers to the integration of gender equality in an interdisciplinary manner across all fields of policy, strategy, research projects, and action plans.

Fig. 9: The Caring City—La Ciudad Cuidadora
Source: María del Mar Muriel

Gender mainstreaming was first introduced as a concept at the United Nations Third World Conference on Women in Nairobi in 1985 and integrated by the Council of Europe as a policy-making strategy in 1998.[170] For urban planning, *gender mainstreaming* means that the gender perspective must be taken into account in all processes, phases, and stages of development.[171] However, analysis conducted in 2019, by an international task force of the Academy for Territorial Development in the Leibniz Association, showed that *gender mainstreaming* had not yet been implemented in spatial planning in EU countries.[172] That a gap exists between setting targets and implementing them in practical terms is of course well known, as is the fact that the topic has taken on greater relevance in what is currently the fourth wave of feminism. Even so, recent European initiatives focusing on architecture and building culture show little evidence of a plan of action for realizing spaces that are equitable from an intersectional feminist perspective. At the global level, gender eqality is included as one of the seventeen goals on the United Nations' 2030 Agenda for Sustainable Development.[173] In 2020 the World Bank published a comprehensive handbook for gender-inclusive planning.[174]

Fig. 10, Pages 82–83: Clips from the opera *A Marvelous Order* on the digital monitors in Times Square, New York City
Source: Ka-Man Tse

Fig. 11, Pages 84–85: Community Garden in Alphabet City on the Lower East Side
Source: Karin Hartmann

Fig. 12, Pages 86–87: Jane-Jacobs-Weg and Janis-Joplin-Promenade in the Seestadt Aspern district of Vienna
Source: Karin Hartmann

Public and Private Spaces

"Outside of the movies, the needs and wants of girls and young women are almost completely ignored in architecture and planning."[175]
Leslie Kern, *Feminist City*

In 2021, a wave of public protests erupted across London following the kidnap and murder of marketing executive Sarah Everard. Initiatives such as Reclaim These Streets[176] and Everyone's Invited demanded safe spaces for women, immediately gaining enormous popularity. Thousands of women described their experiences of sexualized violence and spoke up about the *rape culture*[177] that characterizes urban public space. The media addressed the issue and launched their own campaigns.[178] *ZEIT Magazin* even collected fifty quotes from female joggers: "I believe that I'm entitled to as much space in public as a man. I likewise belong everywhere," states 50-year-old Anna from Hamburg. An anonymous Berliner notes that she has to repeatedly fight for a place in public space, and that there is almost no awareness of it: "No one pays attention to how the world can be made safer for us."[179] What is striking about the global movement following Everard's murder and the resulting surge of publicity is that women describe not only their experience as victims of sexualized violence, but also increasingly express their rage over the fact that they can't move freely in public space—on the contrary, they feel as if they are being treated like fair game.

The Space That Remains

The app "Safe & the City", developed by the London-based Jillian Kowalchuk, is intended to help women plan a safer route through the city.[180] In fact, the award-winning app generates the safest route by enabling users to document and define the locations of their negative experiences. It ultimately suggests the path with the least probable amount of harassment. Like a negative map, it makes the androcentric city visible: it blackens the spaces that women should avoid. Hence, the day-to-day negative experiences of numerous women engender a cartographic image. The app's slogan—"Get to Your Destination Safely"—not only promises a secure pathway, but it helps others by making one's own experiences public. However, user reviews—such as "This is such a brilliant idea and it makes navigating London feel safe"—raise the question of who is responsible for ensuring that a city's inhabitants are able to use it safely. Whereas discussions in numerous internet forums revolve around whether catcalling is disrespectful, this app makes a business out of the concrete fear of being harassed and violence in public space. For the most part, users are simply relieved that the app "solves" the daily problem with little effort, and that they can finally have a better share in public space. But these reviews also reveal the distressing plight of its female users: "After an attack last year with no help from the police, I feel like I can at least make the journey home safer for people in the area. Brilliant piece of technology!"[181]

In the wake of the protests across London, Boris Johnson pledged to double the funds for surveillance cameras and lighting. However, this promise was apparently made without acknowledging research findings which show that London is already one of most heavily monitored cities in the world. The cameras may lead to the conviction of perpetrators, but they do not prevent crimes. In this respect, cameras are in no way conducive to a woman's sense of security, as revealed in a study by United Nations Women UK.[182] From the perspective of those affected, the promise to make the city safer through increased surveillance is like the prospect of an antenatal class on the subject of contraception. As Leslie Kern points out, women only feel more secure through urban planning measures if other disadvantages are lessened on a social, cultural, and economic level: "... Fear can never simply be 'designed out.'"[183]

During the Covid-19 pandemic, one was able to see in the marketplace how women holding their childrens' hands zig-zagged across the square to dodge the path of others. They wanted to bump into other people even less than usual. The dominant behavior of many men in public spaces reminds women every day that they belong less in certain places: with every walk they take, they experience the dichotomy between public and private space—whereas men, historically seen as "free citizens," are aligned with public space, women tend to be assigned the private. Kern points out how women's fear serves as a form of social control: "It limits our use of public spaces, shapes our choices ... and keeps us ... dependent on men as protectors."[184] The economic impact of the detours women must take due to this fear is largely disregarded. Even for women themselves: in everyday life, the inhospitable city keeps them from using the shortest routes for taking care of their errands.

Women's anger over the restricted use of common ground is growing, and it is becoming visible in many more places. Because they are increasingly being heard, the new visibility of women and other marginalized groups will change society's balance of power. This shift in perspective could also be reflected in terms of space.

Places for Girls and Young Women

The first public space designed for and designated to young women is still in frequent use today: the shopping mall. Economic interests recognized early on that the mall was a site where they could meet women at their own safety level. Unfortunately, the mall continues to be where women feel safest today.[185]

It is no accident that these commercial interests are aimed at monopolizing the attention of young girls and women: as potential future consumers, they constitute an important economic resource. If the classic distribution of roles is maintained in their future partnership, women will most likely be responsible for managing a family's disposable capital, and for deciding what share of the household income—whether generated solely or jointly—is spent on what.[186] The unmanageable expanse of public space is seen as the antithesis of the cozy shopping mall. The extended message that young women shouldn't be alone in public becomes palpable when something bad happens: when something does occur, the question quite often arises as to what the girl was doing there in the first place and how she was dressed—as if it is these factors, and not the perpetrators, that determines their safety.

What public spaces do girls and young women wish for? How do they perceive spaces and appropriate them? In Germany, there currently exists little data that separates these relations according to gender. Through talking with researchers and teachers off the record, the following picture emerges: boys tend to appropriate a substantial amount of space. They prefer places where they can move about in public, for example sandlots. Girls tend to prefer closed spaces, where they can meet and talk to others. Nonetheless, they are seen as "problem" cases, since their demands are often unknown, less obvious, and therefore less "spectacular". What is interesting here is not the basic observation that girls and boys have different approaches, but how these are evaluated. Martina Löw has analyzed the various views of gender-specific activity in space, placing them in historical context.[187] In the 1930s, investigations into the individual appropriation of space by boys and girls verified that they do indeed claim it differently. Boys display excessive, uncontrolled behavior and roam about, often by themselves. By contrast, girls tend to stay in their own area. Reasons are sought for the localized nature of their activity: "What drives the boys to rove and to wander far from their parents' homes was not a question that was asked; expansive spatial behavior seems normal and desirable. The reasons for addressing girls' behavior one-sidedly as a problem are found in the fact that women are symbolically posited to be the Other, to be explained, whereas men's behavior is deemed to be the norm and thus not in need of explanation."[188] Conclusions were—and continue to be—drawn for girls from this "norm". She continues:

"More recently, the finding that boys' range of action is larger has been corroborated repeatedly by very diverse empirical studies. ... And there is a persistent assumption that "a larger space" for girls would be desirable."[189]

Based on this evaluation, programs continue to be developed that are intended to urge girls as well as boys to take up more space, and to move around more in that space. If *othering* is eliminated, it becomes clear that girls are as spatially competent as boys. As Löw points out, they do not appropriate spaces by way of distance, but by way of people. In this respect, space as such is less relevant to them, rather it is the relationships that develop in that space that are of primary importance.[190]

Reumannplatz in Vienna is widely regarded as the result of successful gender-inclusive planning. An obstructed view, plenty of seating and usable space of varying quality, access to public restrooms, and a direct connection to the subway station turn the square into a neighborhood meeting place. Girls and young women helped design it according to their ideas. As part of a competition, a survey was conducted among approximately 280 girls from the age of nine onwards from surrounding schools. On a safety day, the students inspected the square alongside police officers and voiced their needs. In this way, for instance, it was decided that excess vegetation and poorly visible areas were both to be avoided. On other activity days, the girls painted the seating and specifically addressed other issues. The Reumädchenbühne, a stage that the girls requested for their own events, was inaugurated in 2020, and an additional street sign was erected: Reumädchenplatz.[191]

Schooling Perception

The systematic introduction of children and adolescents to the importance of the built environment at the perceptual level has not yet been explicitly embedded in the German educational system. Unlike in other European countries, knowledge and skills regarding spatial perception and design continue to be communicated primarily by volunteers based on their own experience. Currently, there exists neither a professional science nor a specialist didactics.[192] There may be numerous good approaches and building blocks for a curriculum, as well as unconventional, low-threshold access to (and innovative concepts for) optional afternoon courses, but they are yet to be systematically implemented in schools. As such, it is largely left up to chance whether young people encounter the subject during their school career. Various experts are working on closing this gap and on ensuring this content is taught at school, using a multidisciplinary approach where possible. The increasing awareness of the connection between planning and building, and developing solutions to address the climate crisis, might convey a greater sense of urgency in terms of finally putting the subject on the educational agenda. In establishing a professional science and specialist didactics, there also exists the possibility of structuring these in such a way that they are gender-neutral from the very outset. Girls and young women could learn to forge a relationship with the built environment. It would make it possible to instill in them an awareness that their need for space is extremely valuable, and indispensable for the creation of an environment that caters to everybody.

Fig. 13, Pages 96–97: Gender-inclusive Reumannplatz in Vienna
Source: Karin Hartmann

In their project FLICKRUM—Places for Girls, the Swedish architectural office White Arkitekter explored the specific needs of girls and young women with regard to public space. They found that while children up to the age of seven use play areas in equal shares, above the age of eight the number of boys who use them rises to 80 percent, whereas girls increasingly withdraw. All in all, White Arkitekter observed a lack of knowledge around the issue of how public spaces address girls' needs. In a practical exercise, girls built models on a scale of 1:50. The task consisted in them taking a neglected site they knew of and rearranging it into an ideal one. The results show: "Both project and process reveal their preference for public places with strong character concerning colour and form, places for sitting together face to face, protected from weather and wind, to see without necessary be seen [sic], a sense of intimacy without being constrictive; and most of all, to be able to leave an imprint on their city."[193] Given the situation of girls in the public sphere, their desire for a safe haven away from home is hardly surprising.

The genuine interest in which spaces appeal to children and young people of both genders, and the will to realize these as a natural feature of urban life by means of public funds, form the breeding ground for a successful resonance between person and environment. The standpoint on care as an immanent design element, described in the previous chapter, serves here as an important milestone in approaching the challenges of climate change. A new generation that is growing up with built environment education understands care as an implicit responsibility of architecture and planning. This generation will be provided with the relevant knowledge about how they themselves can slow down global warming and possibly transform it into an interesting line of work, which would directly benefit the profession.

A Self-Reflexive Professional Discourse

*"The numbers of women actually practicing
is far fewer than of women in school.
How do we explain that as a discipline?
How can we not be concerned about it?
We have to be concerned about it."*[194]
Monica Ponce de Leon, MPdL Studio

For a long time, questions concerning equal opportunity in the field
of architecture were met with the statement: it's about the resulting
quality, irrespective of who builds it. This correlated neatly with the
"monochrome" self-image of the architect, in which all characteristics of one's personality must take up a subordinate role to work.
Conversely, this claim also meant that, for the most part, predominantly white male architects were in a position to plan and build
high-quality architecture, an attitude that overlooked the causes and
effects of systemic discrimination. For many years, falling back on a
debate over quality prevented the professional discourse from even
perceiving a problem in the first place.
For the United States, Despina Stratigakos wrote in 2016 that the
silence over gender issues in architecture "is particularly astonishing
at a time when the status of women has become a public relations
nightmare for the profession, with a deluge of negative stories

appearing in the press and online blogs".[195] The situation in the United States cannot be applied 1:1, in particular since the nightmare of negative media coverage in Germany and Europe was largely absent. In the meantime, this silence is now subsiding and the debate is currently taking a decisive step forward. Once awareness of the complex problems surrounding "women in architecture" was given a voice in special issues and anthologies centering on women architects, the exhibition "Frau Architekt"—organized in 2017 by the Deutsches Architekturmuseum (DAM; German Architecture Museum)—also marked the starting point for a differentiated analysis of the topic.[196] The "Gendergerechte Architektur" (Gender-Balanced Architecture) issue of *Bauwelt* in 2021 and the "Zeitgenössische feministische Raumpraxis" (Comtemporary Feminist Spatial Practice) issue of *ARCH+* in 2021 finally placed content-related focus on the connections between architecture, gender, and space. The integration of the findings of feminist research into "classic" professional discourse can catalyze change that is urgently required for further development of the professional culture toward a more intersectional and context-oriented perspective.

Media as Loudspeakers
In the chapter "Learning Architecture," the method described for filling design professorships—not according to academic qualifications but from professional practice—supports more of a self-referential professional discourse. Professional media play a pivotal role in this respect, since professional success is measured by competition awards as well as by executed and published works.[197] Specialist journals, online magazines, blogs, and publications work as loudspeakers: continuous coverage of a work is a marker for success and recognition, and hence a prerequisite for the success of the office and for subsequent professorships, awards, and invitations to competitions. If the office is already established, media coverage contributes to maintaining this level of success.
Despina Stratigakos furthermore singles out the monograph, in particular in history, as an elementary means of portraying the

"architect in a lineage of 'great men,'" in which collaboration with a partner was frequently neglected: "[The monograph] continues to be the bible of the star system." With the monograph, architects—in part personally—inscribe themselves in history. She acknowledges that the monograph is increasingly losing its powerful effect, because perspectives are changing.[198]

To what extent does specialist media reflect or reinforce gender roles? Do they contribute to the continuation or maintenance of the status quo in the sector?

A random evaluation of specialist journals from 2016 and 2021/22 indicates how the visual representation of women and the participation of female authors has changed over a period of six years. An analysis was conducted of all photos in which people were depicted. This resulted in the following picture: among all of the journalists, the share of women averaged 29 percent; among the overall number of people depicted, 28 percent of them were female. Of these, 90 percent were shown in a passive situation, be it as a "decorative accessory," a passer-by or in the position of listener. Meanwhile, 75 percent of the images showed men, 88 percent of them in an active position, be it as the author or engaged in an activity. The picture has already changed in 2021/22. Whereas 39 percent of the contributions were written by women, they are depicted in 53 percent of the photos of people, and are in a passive position in only 63 percent of them. By contrast, men can be seen in 84 percent of the images, but only 62 percent of them are in an active position.

To an alarming extent, the media continue to present the status quo with various role expectations. What is particularly noticeable are advertising clients, which almost consistently make use of these stereotypes. It begins with an architect with an angular face and graying hair, and ends with the depiction of women as an alleged surprise effect.

Specialist media assume a substantial role in the framing of professional culture. As the "loudspeakers" of the architectural sector they have the potential to give women and other marginalized groups more space and more of a voice as part of a natural progression

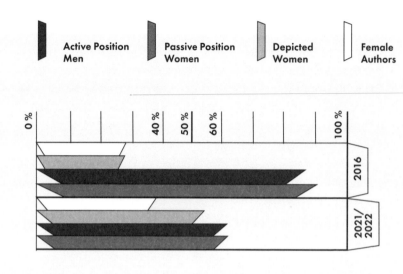

Active Position Men

Passive Position Women

Depicted Women

Female Authors

Fig. 14: Depiction of women and men with a share of women authors
in specialist architectural journals in 2016 and 2021/22
Source: Analysis: Karin Hartmann/Infographic: PAPINESKA

toward parity. Some specialist media still bear male identifiers in their name and hence perpetuate a tradional image. The renaming, in 2022, of the journal published by the Association of German Architects (BDA) from *der architekt* to *Die Architekt* may be seen as an elegant example of this reframing.

Countermovements

For a long time, equal opportunity was considered a clear and consensual aim of social development. Since the onset of the Covid-19 pandemic, the increasing awareness of what role gender plays in various socio-political as well as economic developments has triggered discernible countermovements. Dr. Alexandra Scheele, a lecturer for the sociology of work and economics, explains: "We are seeing … that the consensus on what gender equality means today has become fragile." As a possible cause she cites the fact that crises often bring about an increased need for security, and that fixed gender roles may communicate a greater sense of security with respect to one's own role in society.[199]

This is demonstrated most clearly by the discord in the debate surrounding the gendering of language. In May 2020, the first broadcast on public television in which *Steuerzahler:innen* (male:female taxpayers) was spoken with a glottal stop, provoked a storm of indignation. Right-wing populist and conservative parties and media make strategic use of this commotion around gender issues, and in doing so hamper important discussions about its content.[200]

Reactions in specialist architectural media tend to follow similar patterns. In 2021, for instance, in an article entitled "Die neuen Chefinnen" (The New Women Bosses) for the *Deutsches Architektenblatt*, Kerstin Kunekath provides detailed introductions to three architectural offices led by women.[201] Two issues later, four letters to the editor were printed. Two women readers welcomed the article and shared aspects of their own biographies. Through the reactions of letters written by male readers, however, one gradually understands the mechanisms deployed to call into question the relevance of the article. As a single father, an independent architect did not feel addressed by the discussion. In challenging the justification of the overall account, he made use of the "not-all-men argument": generalized statements about privilege, based on statistics, are set against an individual perspective—however infrequent it may be. As a result, the respective discussion is called into question. The second letter from a male reader perceived the article as "old-white-man-bashing" and complained that its portrayal discriminated against him. His reaction may be understandable on an individual basis, but it fails to acknowledge who can be discriminated against and who cannot.[202]

In 2021, Wolfgang Thierse reacted against news coverage that referred to him as an "old white man."[203] He insisted on being categorized according to arguments only and not based on his membership of a particular social group. This is precisely what happens to marginalized groups from childhood onwards, often lasting their entire lives. Those who experience discrimination are surprised by the knee-jerk reactions of the most privileged members of society when they get a taste of how it feels to be pigeonholed exclusively on the basis of gender, ethnic membership, or age. However, their experience is incomparable: they do not suffer structural or institutional discrimination—on the contrary, they have been historically privileged for their characteristics, and continue to be advantaged worldwide. Despite having the same qualifications, *they* are the ones who statistically tend to get the job and the apartment. The second letter from a male reader goes on say that, ultimately, success is a question of mutual respect and recognition of the accomplishments of our elders. It is exactly this respect that women and other marginalized groups lack in the area of architecture and which has led to the current imbalance. In the end, he criticizes the article's tone and, in doing so, attempts to deny its relevance altogether. *Silencing* serves to relativize or ridicule supposedly uncomfortable opinions with the aim of quashing them.[204] The reader's letter is a striking example of what is surely in part an unconscious counter-reaction to unexpected changes; it certainly does not reflect the entire stance of the "classic" professional discourse on the ongoing development of equal opportunity.

In the professional as well as social debates over gender, there are numerous voices reflective of both genders which address these grievances and make them public. In *ZEIT Magazin*, the journalist Christian Gesellmann writes laconically about sexism and his own role: "The mere fact of being a white cis man commenting on the subject of sexism is apparently sufficient to be asked to be an author. While my girlfriend cleans the apartment. She is also an author and certainly has more to say about the subject of sexism than I do, but here I sit, I get the contract that she doesn't get, and I get the remuneration she doesn't."[205] The reactions in the comments column are analogous to the letters from readers in the *Deutsches Architektenblatt*. Many women express their appreciation for the empathetic point of view but most men, on the other hand, distance themselves: they do not share the problems and thoughts expressed by the author, and feel sorry for him.

It will be interesting to see where the social debate goes and how it will tie into the professional debate. What is promising is not only the fact that women and other underprivileged groups gain more media presence in the future but, above all, that they are listened to.

Exhibitions

In 2012, the exhibition "Der Architekt: Geschichte und Gegenwart eines Berufsstandes" (The Architect: History and Present of a Profession) at the Architekturmuseum in Munich, curated by Winfried Nerdinger, was highly popular, as it represented the entire body of work of German architects and reflected on the profession more broadly— albeit extremely one-sidedly: of the total of 816 pages in the illustrated catalogue, all of sixteen were devoted to women architects. In their article on female architectural history, authors Regine Maasberg and Ute Prinz conclude: "The profession has not yet restructured planning and building ... into new and most of all sustainable, social, and practical constellations. The motto appears to be: Be passionate about architecture, or not at all."[206] Hence, the exhibition itself bears witness to the one-dimensional perspective of the profession. Today, just ten years later, such an exhibition would no longer be possible. The voices of women architects, their works, research projects, and publications, have become too loud, diverse, and interesting. The first solo exhibition of the work of a female architect to be presented at the Architekturmuseum since its founding in 1976 was Lina Bo Bardi in 2014. This has been followed by numerous solo exhibitions at Europe's architeture museums and centers, which will only continue in the future.

Ambivalent Competition Culture

Architecture and planning competitions are considered a traditional instrument for the acquisition of exciting public building projects. In open competitions, young offices—insofar as they exist—take advantage of their chance of a breakthrough by winning a competition. The credo of anonymity, equal treatment, and transparency illustrates the central values of the procedure.[207] However, in view of 150 years of competition culture, the question arises to what extent this has itself contributed to, and perpetuates, the pronounced gender inequality in architecture.

Several successful women architects were awarded their first major contracts through having won a competition and were able to base the future of their office and, indirectly, their later careers on it. Nevertheless, as already alluded to in the chapter "Learning Architecture," competitions also work based on existing narratives of the profession, including an overtime culture that goes hand in hand with the dissolution of boundaries between job and private life. Participation is possible only if the corresponding time and monetary resources are available. An exceptional circumstance lasting a number of weeks is neither readily organizable nor financeable for couples who have an equal share of care work, nor for single fathers. In this respect, the time has come to also critically challenge this practice in terms of discrimination within professional culture. Who benefits from participating and succeeding in competitions? Who cannot participate?

In their manifesto, the international Architecture Lobby also advocates the elimination of work without pay in the architectural field. Unpaid competitions reinforce structural inequalities generated by factors such as race, class, and gender: "Architecture is work."[208] What role does the jury play, for example? It is an open secret that juries cannot always be impartial and that their procedures are therefore not anonymous in all areas. The drawing and rendering style of many offices is their trademark and has high recognition value. This often means that despite an anonymous procedure the jury is, off the record, familiar with the authors of the submissions and that their contributions can also be favored accordingly. Low-threshold access to major planning contracts, which is essentially something of a given in the case of open competitions *qua* procedure, can be limited by these practices. It is obvious that this largely invisible practice promotes existing structures and that women and other marginalized groups can be at a disadvantage.[209] The implementation of blind auditions for orchestras, for example, has substantially increased the share of women musicians. Despite their long tradition, planning competitions have thus far not had a comparable effect on the gender balance in architecture. It is not merely a matter of revising the procedure, but rather of recognizing discriminatory factors in order to rule them out. The goal of any analysis of biased aspects of competition procedure should instead be to take advantage of competitions as an instrument for increasing diversity and for improving access.

Because on the other hand, competitions offer good opportunities for keeping in mind gender-specific needs within planning from the very beginning. The announcement provides an opportunity to analyze the needs of a specific site and for systematically incorporating them into the performance requirements, the usage requirements, and ultimately into a spatial program. In collaboration with its Fachfrauenbeirat (Professional Women's Council), Berlin's Senatsverwaltung für Stadtentwicklung (Senate Administration for Urban Development) published the guideline "Gender Mainstreaming in der Stadtentwicklung" (Gender Mainstreaming in Urban Development), in which it makes concrete recommendations for how the gender perspective can be integrated into the task, among other things.[210] The Zentrum Frau in Beruf und Technik (Center for Women in Career and Technology) published the tool "Gender Mainstreaming für Planungswettbewerbe" (Gender Mainstreaming for Planning Competitions), which outlines how a gendered perspective might be better implemented throughout the individual steps of a competition.[211] In their guideline "Gender Mainstreaming," the City of Vienna established a matrix for the preliminary review of competition submissions with regard to gender, which gives hints for each specific building project.[212] Equal representation in jury sessions plus the representation of gender competence is recommended in several guidelines. Equal representation does not mean one-third women.

Award Procedures

Historically, architecture prizes and awards are given to male candidates at a ratio of approximately 80 to 90 percent.[213] The debate over the gender balance of the Pritzker Prize has not subsided since its presentation in 1991 to Robert Venturi and the resistance articulated by his partner, Denise Scott Brown. An increasing number of women have been receiving architectural prizes over the last decade. In the United States, the *Architectural Record* presents the Women in Architecture Award in five categories. Moreover, in North America, further awards are conferred by foundations and universities. In the United Kingdom, the W Awards are presented in one national and one international category.[214] France also has an architecture prize for women spanning several different categories.[215] Further awards are presented in Italy and in Iraq. In Germany, the association Diversity in Architecture was founded with the goal of awarding an international architeture prize for women. The first one is planned for 2023. In 2016, Despina Stratigakos observed that there is greater openness for women's awards in the field of architecture: "A decade ago, the establishment of women-centered prizes would have been greeted with less openness ... . But the recent outspokenness about discrimination in the profession has generated a newfound sense of solidarity and even pride in that identity."[216]

Women's Networks

A trend within architectural practice is professional networks for women planners. If they are involved in professional policy, they compete along with other professional associations in electing the representative in the national chambers of architects. For more than thirty years, the architektinnen initiative Nordrhein-Westfalen (ai nw) has been a career network for female civil engineers, urban planners, and architects of all disciplines. It is likewise active in the area of professional policy and has had a representative in the Assembly of Representatives of the Chamber of Architecture of North Rhine-Westphalia since 2000. Whereas for fifteen years the ai nw occupied between eight and fifteen of 201 seats, in 2020 its share of seats doubled to thirty, and it became the third-strongest association. It won votes with its themes "Gender Pay Gap" and "Auf Wiedersehen in die Elternzeit" ("Parental Leave-Taking," but with the ironic overtone that once a new mother takes leave, she never returns to her job). What is notable is that, with its 150 members, the ai nw received a total of 1,738 votes: a clear indication that numerous female planners seek resolution of their concerns with respect to professional policy. This is not simply a special case for North Rhine-Westphalia: besides the ai nw, in recent years other women's planning networks involved in architectural policy have been able to increase their number of representatives in the respective chambers, such as the Baufrauen from Nuremberg and n-ails from Berlin.

The use of women's networks affords female planners an opportunity to support each other without competition along gender lines. The exchange of information concerning practical issues, the mutual recommendation to juries and committees, lectures and commissions, and the will to eliminate gender-related injustices in the workplace can support women architects in any position in their everyday professional life.

The analysis of the history of the network Planung Architektur Frauen (PAF) in Switzerland constitutes a profound basis for the founding of such networks, and for their structures.[217]

Parallel Structures

Student-led initiatives that hold a lot of promise for the transformation of educational perspectives and structures have been established internationally within a short period of time. At the Eidgenössische Technische Hochschule Zürich (ETH; Swiss Federal Institute of Technology Zurich), the Parity Group conducted the Parity Talks for the seventh time in 2022. The group originated in 2014 with the goal of putting the university's lack of diversity with respect to race, class, and gender at the top of their agenda. Within a short time, initiatives with similar goals were founded at other universities: 2019 saw the founding of the collective Claiming*Spaces at the Technische Universität Wien (TU Wien; Technical University of Vienna) and the Parity Board at the Technische Universität München (TUM; Technical University of Munich), as well as the DRAGlab and the École Polytechnique Fédérale de Lausanne in 2021.[218] The parent organization, Parity Front, founded in 2020, connects the initiatives; these likewise include networks like Womxn in Design at the Harvard Graduate School of Design, and Womxn in Design and Architecture at Princeton University.

The initiatives operate in close connection with one another, via social media, digital and analog events as well as joint publications. Using various formats, they cultivate an intersectional, feminist discourse, at universities in particular. It will be exciting to see whether these new initiatives successfully institutionalize themselves and, in terms of perspective, make their demands visible with respect to professional policy.

Along with other tendencies, the increase in the number of awards for architecture and the attractiveness of women's networks speaks to the development of structures parallel to the mainstream architectural discourse. Women—whether of color, white or Black—are rapidly developing their own content, networks, teaching, and action practices, in the area of education as well as professional practice. Whereas the dropout rate of women leaving architecture as a career may have led to them being excluded as architects in the statistics, they are now exercising influence over new content and discourses that are emerging out of neighboring institutions, foundations, and educational practices, as well as their own initiatives. They also make a substantial contribution to greater interdisciplinarity, as Torsten Lange points out: "Many of the currently most interesting internationally networked actors and groups whose works are based on an intersectional, queer, and feminist approach explore the potential of critical and expanded practice in the area of architecture, knowing full well that they are denied mainstream acceptance and respectability."[219]

Fig. 15, Page 114: Poster for the Parity Talks III 2018
Source: Parity Group/Original Photo Courtesy OMA,
Design by Völlm+Walthert

ROLE MODELS

PARITY TALKS III

Symposium und Diskussionsanlass zu Fragen der Gender Parity im
Kontext der Ausbildung und des Berufs von Architektinnen und Architekten
bzw. Planerinnen und Planern.
Symposium and discussion forum surrounding the issue of gender
parity within the architectural and planning disciplines.

8. MÄRZ / MARCH 2018, 9:00

VORTRAGENDE / SPEAKERS:

Inge Beckel
Architekturpublizistin

Maria Conen
TU Munich / Conen Sigl Architekten

Kathrin Dörfler
ITA / ETH Zürich

Isabelle Fehlmann
ILA / ETH Zürich

Romina Grillo
UNULAUNU / ETH Zürich

Mike Guyer
Gigon/Guyer Architekten / ETH Zürich

**Almut Grunewald &
Bettina Zimmermann**
gta Archiv / ETH Zürich

Marcela Hanáčková
gta / ETH Zürich

Rixt Hoekstra
Design Academy Eindhoven

Andreas Kalpakci
gta / ETH Zürich

Torsten Lange
gta / ETH Zürich

Anna-Maria Meister
Princeton

Sarah Nichols
gta / ETH Zürich

**Eliana Perotti &
Katia Frey**
ETH Wohnforum / ETH Zürich

**Anna Luise Schubert &
Amelie Wegner**
Bauhaus University Weimar

Romila Storjohann
Equal! / ETH Zürich

ETHzürich

DARCH

National Centre of Competence
in Research
Digital Fabrication

e**Q**ual!
Equal Opportunities for Women and Men

INTERNAL GUESTS:
Susana Ana
Wolf Boen
Britta Hentschel
Charlotte Malterre-Barthes
Jasmin Mahli
Christopher Metz
Daniela Ortiz dos Santos
Gabrielle Schaad
Laila Seewang
Gieron Sievi
Philip Ursprung

Eine Veranstaltung der Parity Group
am Departement Architektur.
An event organised by the Parity
Group at the Department of
Architecture, organised jointly
supported by D-ARCH
AAA & architektur.ch

contact@arch.ethz.ch

ETH HÖNGGERBERG, ROTE HÖLLE, HIL

The new actors use their voices politically. The WAI Think Tank and Architecture Lobby make demands and have clear ideas of how the sector has to be transformed.[220]

In this respect, the self-efficacy of the work of women architects and other marginalized groups within and outside of the professional discourse in architecture has substantially changed. They are not asking for participation but are forming their own networks and creating their own discourses. In the medium term, it remains to be seen whether both discourses merge to become one, or whether they become parallel structures.

In Conversation with Afaina de Jong

Afaina de Jong is a Dutch architect and scholar. With her studio AFARAI in Amsterdam she implements approaches from research and theory, grounded in an intersectional feminist practice. AFARAI questions the relationship between architecture and space in terms of its social impact. De Jong directs the master's degree program for Contextual Design at the Design Academy Eindhoven and, in 2021, was a guest professor at the Claiming*Spaces collective at Vienna's technical university, TU Wien. Together with Het Nieuwe Instituut and Debra Solomon, she curated the Netherlands' contribution to the 2021 Venice Architecture Biennale. In response to the theme proposed by the Biennale's General Commissioner and Curator Hashim Sarkis, "How will we live together?", de Jong posed the question: "Who is We?" With its project The Multiplicity of Other, AFARAI explored the many perspectives inherent in a "we" through the form of an installation and a variety of interdisciplinary approaches.

KARIN HARTMANN: *Afaina, in your work as an architect and as a teacher you address the issue of a lack of diversity and its effects. Why do you think the profession of architecture is so male dominated? Why do women—whether Black or of color, white or Indigenous—leave architecture, or why are they underrepresented in the profession?*

AFAINA DE JONG: It's a general issue that plays out in many professions in society—that first and foremost. But then, what is weird in architecture is that in the schools we start with 50:50. And when you look again, ten years after graduation, only 10 to 20 percent of the women remain in the profession. So, there is something particular going on in architecture. I've talked to so many women about it. I think it's a mixture of things in a way. On the one hand, there's always a lot of talk about women being able to pursue motherhood and combine it with a career in architecture. That part is sometimes hard, because of the work culture. At the same time, you also want to practice in a field where your opinion is valued and where you have a certain degree of agency. Those things are maybe lacking. Often, your expertise is questioned, for instance, by colleagues or contractors or building managers. And that can be quite demotivating. What we're talking about in general is a sense of agency, finding a place where you belong, where you can thrive. And if the culture within the practice is not one in which women can thrive, then, of course, they're going to leave. Which is a shame, because I think architecture—ideally speaking—is a perfect profession to take in many different directions.

What do you mean by that?

You can become a writer, a designer, you can become an analyst or a researcher, you can choose to go in so many ways career-wise. So, I'd also like to urge everyone active in our field to see that a lot of talent is getting lost because of women and marginalized groups dropping out, which I think is really a big issue.

What is your vision for changing the situation in the architectural field and culture? How can we overcome the current system?
Well, it should happen on multiple levels. First of all, it has to start within education. We develop this culture of working really long, late hours, which is gruesome. Studio work, late nights, deadlines— we cultivate that already when we're in school. That's being perpetuated by people who graduate and then set up their own practices, but it's also adopted by the offices.

We should start reinventing how best to work on architectural projects together efficiently, or maybe not even efficiently. Maybe from a perspective of caring for each other. What would that look like? How would we then structure our week, and how would that translate into the offices? Secondly, in education, too, it's weird. When I was studying, there were no female professors that ever taught me. Sometimes I hear even women architects say, "Yeah, I don't know. I don't know where to find them." The women. Or the others. But they are there. They are in the schools. But maybe they're not right *there* there, so you don't know how to reach them, and maybe they're not interested in your working environment, right? Because your environment doesn't invite them in or doesn't attract them— because it is so "singular," so one-dimensional in its perspective. So, I also think studios and offices should re-evaluate how they can draw any of the new talent in, because those people are there. It's not that they are not there. We have to be active.

In your article in the magazine ARCH+,[221] you write a letter to the American feminist, poet, and civil rights activist Audre Lorde (1934–1992) in which you quote her famous essay: "The master's tools will never dismantle the master's house."[222] But if we can't use our old tools for building a new system—which new instruments do we need for initiating change? What do you think is the next urgent step we need to take?
That's a very big question. There are probably a thousand different things to do. Of course, that's a very famous idea of hers. What stands out for me, is that often we're talking about diversity or inclusivity

but still thinking from the standpoint of being in a dominant system and letting some people in. You know, like, let's make a little place for adding them to the same framework and using the same tools to do that, just stretching it. One of the things that I addressed with my work in the Netherlands Pavilion at the 2021 Venice Architecture Biennale is that we can also approach the reality in which we live as one member of a multiplicity. There are many, many practices out there that are doing things differently. You can see that already, for instance, there is so much insistence now on Indigenous knowledge. I think we just should become more aware of all these other methods. Methods that are outside of our profession, or forms of knowledge that lie outside of our practices. You need all that knowledge to make sense of this very complex world. You just have to realize that all the skills and the tools you learned in architecture school are part of a very specific set, a set called modernism.

Why modernism?

Outside of modernism, for centuries, so many different ways of doing things, of approaching or solving problems, creating community or even building, have existed and still exist. It would definitely be a beginning to be able to see and value that. What if architecture education wasn't so violent anymore with its feedback? What if it was more about asking questions, or was approached from a place of rest, or a place of care? That would be so different. Care for each other and care for the people that we design for, but also care for the people who build, for instance. You know, there are so many bad labor practices within architecture. If we even want to begin to design with a view toward care? We have to address that. There are so many things that need to be changed within our own profession.

Do you think it's necessary to rebuild, or to recast, the so-called mainstream discourse in architecture, or do you instead see these debates and structures as running parallel to those of the mainstream?

The parallel structures are already there, right? We're just not engaging with them. We're in our own little bubble, which is super comfortable but at the same time also makes it very hard for us to be relevant, because the complexities are becoming so great. I, myself, am very interested in blending different parallel realities and ways of doing things "otherwise"—that is, in another way—in our discourse and way of working. I like that kind of otherwise. Like, "how do you do it otherwise?" Maybe that's just a question you'll always have to ask yourself. Or I feel, because of where I grew up or the people I grew up with, that I see a lot of different things, or approach architectural assignments differently because I have different knowledge that maybe some of my peers don't have. And I think that's good [laughs]. And I must say, when I was a student, I was not appreciated. Often, responses from instructors were more like: "Yeah, this is ridiculous. This has nothing to do with reality." Well, not with your reality. But for many, many people, it is reality. For me, it is all about value. Issues like lived experience, for instance, have not been valued that much. Although I think it has been valued in some women's architectural works. They often had no choice but to design nice kitchens, but still, that also came from a lived experience, like the Frankfurt kitchen. We should implement that kind of methodology to listen to lived experience. I think it's super. Valuing things otherwise—again, in a way that we haven't before.

What advice do you give your female, Black, and/or Indigenous students to survive within the system?
Yeah, that's a good one. I mean, not everyone will survive. The question is: do you want to be in the system? I think you first have to ask yourself: is this the place where I can make a difference?
Or should you just be opportunistic about it and say: "Okay, but I really need the diploma to be able to work as an architect and go my own way afterwards."
I think you must be very aware of the environment in which you find yourself. Also, the things that you'll encounter often have nothing

to do with you personally but are more systemic in a way. But I feel, too, that students nowadays are way more critical and aware; they are, again, active, and really questioning many things. And they're not taking any shit. Sometimes, when I look back, I'm amazed at some of the things that we let slide, while, with my students now, I see that they're super on top of things. They're really saying no to sexism or racism within their educational structures. And hopefully, you know, more teachers and department heads will come in who support this kind of educational change.

But who has been your role model then?
That's very funny.

In architecture.
Yeah, nobody. I mean.

Nobody?
No, no, I wouldn't say nobody, but strangely enough, I don't know, I don't think I really had any architectural role models. Of course, I found Rem Koolhaas very interesting, because he was crossing genres, like his interdisciplinarity is what I really liked. And then I liked Zaha, because she developed a new formal language, completely outside of that kind of modernist mindset that says, "this must be a box." I also really liked the new wave of young Dutch architects at the time, for instance NL Architects, because they were just adding humor to the profession. In terms of having some female or Black role models within architecture, I never really had that. There are now more diverse role models to be inspired by. At the same time, my role models were often outside of architecture. They either came from music, fashion, or writing. I never felt that a role model had to be someone who is active in the exact same field as me. I was interested in crossing all of these boundaries, and in seeing music or fashion or pop culture as information that is needed to be able to understand the contemporary world. And, in that sense, to be able to understand design. Like, what should the ar-

chitecture of a particular design be? How do we engage with each other as a community, and how do you design for that? For me, this sort of approach includes seeing architecture as part of that culture, part of popular culture or mainstream culture or underground culture, of counterculture. Yes, I think I was raised in counterculture. So therefore, how can architecture represent underground culture or counterculture?

How do you live your intersectional approach in your own professional life?
Well, in my professional life, I try to apply it to myself. To position myself, to be aware of and understand the particular context in which I find myself—be it contemporary society or the profession. To see what my privileges are, or what I have riding against me. Likewise, I try to apply the same kind of intersectional framework to the people I'm designing for. To better understand their relationship to power and to a lack of power. So, I really like the framework of intersectionality because it is not black or white. It has many, many layers.

What would you say is for you the most interesting development in contemporary architecture and urban design at the moment?
A couple of things. I like that we are beginning to consider the non-human in a way. At the same time, I think there is still so much to be gained within the human world, because we have excluded so many different ways of life for so long. But I think we cannot do it without also taking nonhuman species into account, especially with this ecological disaster that is now upon us.
And then, very generally, I am super excited about Lesley Lokko being the new curator for the 2023 Venice Architecture Biennale.

It's so fantastic.
OH MY GOD! She is going to be amazing! So, I am super excited about that.

I read an interview with her yesterday and really loved it. She mentioned she was so tired of diversity commissions, which only talk about change but don't actually change anything. That aspect very clearly mirrors the lack of diversity in institutions, at least to me. I imagine she'll really come up with a new perspective—I'm very curious about that.

Yes. I've never met her but hope to meet her and hang out with her. I'm just like, "I want to be friends!" [*laughs*] She probably has friends already, but who knows? I'd love to get to know her.

That sounds great.

Afaina, what are we talking about in, say, thirty years? What do you foresee?

What are we talking about? It's hard to say. That would be roughly 2050, the year the European Union is supposed to be completely carbon neutral. I really hope we make it. We're either going to be talking about how to design for climate disaster, for floods, fires, and earthquakes, or we're going to be designing for how to get off this planet. I don't know. I hope it's going to be more positive than that. Hopefully, we can really be living in a more equitable world, ecologically and socially. Thirty years sounds far in the future, but major change only happens over a long period of time.

Yes, that's true.

So, I do not know. I hope it's not going to be too bleak [*laughs*]. Because I also like that we're talking about feminism and all these things in architecture. It is much needed, especially if we want to solve some of the major problems. At the same time, I'm sometimes so disappointed that we still have to address the issue of equality at a time when we have this major climate disaster pending. I can't help but think, man, we should've dealt with this already. Hopefully, it won't be too late. We shall see.

Thank you so much for your time and your insights, Afaina.

Perspective

Architecture's professional culture and other structural factors, including subtle discrimination and exclusionary narratives, signal to women and other marginalized groups that it has no room for them. In abdicating from the industry, they are simply taking good care of themselves: avoiding work situations that demand absurdly high levels of effort and adjustment that soon become intolerable. Their collective decision to turn their backs on architecture and abandon a profession they love should be seen as a reflection on the system itself. It indicates—and the American Institute of Architects study confirms this—that something is fundamentally wrong in the architecture industry in terms of equal opportunity. If the industry, including its teaching, institutions, practice, and media landscape, truly wants to place a higher value on gender balance and diversity, then it must lay its own foundations, and create a framework that will support this at all levels.

Audre Lorde's famous expression, "The master's tools will never dismantle the master's house,"[223] articulates in a single sentence how new perspectives demand a new system. With systemic change comes new forms of content and modes of practice—in light of the major tasks ahead, this is both a promising and viable prospect. This is especially desirable for architecture because, for many, the current constraints of its professional culture have become unsustainable. Hopefully, thirty years from now, we will be able to see the shift in the industry's culture reflected in our homes, cities, and landscapes.

Glossary

Dimensions of discrimination

The researcher and founder of the Center for Intersectional Justice in Berlin, Dr. Emilia Roig, refers to four dimensions of discrimination, which are mutually dependent and reinforce one another: individual, structural, institutional, and historical discrimination. According to Roig, individual discrimination occurs in personal interactions between people, for example overtly sexist or racist insults. By contrast, structural discrimination constitutes the skeleton of our society, for example by means of laws and funding structures that uphold discrimination. Institutional discrimination denotes the sum of individual decisions and actions of

Bias

A study by the American Institute of Architects/The Center for WorkLife Law, "The Elephant in the (Well-Designed) Room," examined *bias* in the architecture profession and defines the term as follows: "A simple definition of bias is when two otherwise identical people are treated differently because of their membership in a social group; indeed, bias is often measured by giving people identical resumes and documenting how people from different social groups are treated differently."

Care

The term *care* as used in this book is oriented toward the definition formulated by Joan C. Tronto and Berenice Fisher in 1990: "In the most general sense, care [is] *a species activity that includes everything that we do to maintain, continue, and repair our 'world' so that we can live in it as well as possible.* That world includes our bodies, our selves, and our environment, all of which we seek to interweave in a complex, life-sustaining web."[224]

people in powerful positions, for instance in public institutions. Historical discrimination, on the other hand, reveals how past systems continue to influence the present.[225] By definition, the discrimination of privileged groups does not go beyond individual discrimination, since it has no systemic basis and hence cannot have any corresponding impact.

Gender Planning

Gender Planning implements the concept of Gender Mainstreaming at all spatial levels.

Intersectionality and intersectional feminism

The term was coined in the late 1980s by Kimberlé Crenshaw when addressing the fact that, for example, Black women are affected by overlapping discrimination consisting of sexism and racism. On the website of the Center for Intersectional Justice, intersectionality is defined as follows: "The concept of intersectionality describes the ways in which systems of inequality based on gender, race, ethnicity, sexual orientation, gender identity, disability, class and other forms of discrimination 'intersect' to create unique dynamics and effects. For example, when a Muslim woman wearing the Hijab is being discriminated against,

Othering

In an article published by the Goethe Institut, *othering* is explained as follows: "We speak of othering when a person or group is constructed as an other by being positioned as different to an implicit norm. Othering is a process that ascribes an inherent difference or strangeness to a group or an individual, and makes hierarchical distinctions on the basis of that ascription. This act of demarcation has real consequences, because it happens within existing, unequal power structures: those who do the othering speak and act from positions of power, to mark those they deem unlike themselves other. ... For example, there are racist or homophobic descriptions that have established it would be impossible to dissociate her female* from her Muslim identity and to isolate the dimension(s) causing her discrimination. All forms of inequality are mutually reinforcing and must therefore be analysed and addressed simultaneously to prevent one form of inequality from reinforcing another. For example, tackling the gender pay gap alone—without including other dimensions such as race, socio-economic status and immigration status—will likely reinforce inequalities among women."[226]

The goal of intersectional feminism is to end any form of discrimination and to prevent different forms of discrimination—against *race*, class, and gender—being played off against each other.

themselves as negative or offensive in order to sanction identities or behaviors that do not conform to the norm. Othering thus explains that discrimination is an exercise of power that works with labeling and defining groups of people and reducing them to these reductive stereotypes."[227]

Privileges

In the "Glossar gegen die Angst vor Wörtern" (Glossary against the Fear of Words) in *Missy Magazine*, privileges are explained as follows: "Depending on context, privileges are differently arranged advantages that a person enjoys. These include positions such as being *white*, male, cisgender, endowed with capital, or able-bodied. Depending on the initial privileges a person has, it is possible to acquire further privileges over time—for example, economic or in terms of education. ... As a *white* person, it is a privilege to not experience racism; as a wealthy person, it can be a privilege to be protected against poverty. ... What is remarkable is that most privileges are not earned but part of one's personal biography.

Silencing/Hate speech

As part of *hate speech* on the internet, *silencing* is regarded as a strategy to silence certain opinions in discussions. Johannah Lea Illgner analyzed how *hate speech* and *silencing* work together. *Hate speech* is not directed against individuals but against persons as members of a group identity. In particular, in cases of what are perceived as "emotive issues" like feminism and racism, *silencing* by means of vilification, humiliation, and personal attacks successfully ensures that disagreeable opinions are eliminated from the public debate as part of public space. "Dissidents are meant to be intimidated and silenced, thereby 'maintaining' the status quo and, for instance, holding on to the 'traditional' understanding

As a result, they are taken for granted by those who enjoy them."[228]

Rape culture

In its glossary, the European Institute for Gender Equality (EIGE) defines *rape culture* as follows: "Complex of beliefs that encourages male sexual aggression and supports violence against women."
It continues: "It describes a society where violence is seen as sexy and sexuality as violent. Manifestations of a rape culture include instances of sexual violence that range from sexual remarks to sexual touching to rape, as well as condoning such violence against women and presenting it as normal."[229]

of gender roles, sexuality, nationality, etc."[230] Illgner goes on to write that the disappearance of specific opinions and positions in public debates and discourses through silencing constitutes a major legitimacy problem for plural and diverse discussion.[231]

The glossaries of the EIGE, the collective Claiming* Spaces of the Technische Universität Wien, and *Missy Magazine* can be recommended as sources of additional definitions concerning equality issues and discrimination.

Endnotes

1   Anna Heringer, cit. in Katharina Rudolph, "Die Haus-Frauen," *Frankfurter Allgemeine Zeitung*, October 15, 2020, https://www.faz.net/aktuell/stil/quarterly/talentierte-architektinnen-zu-gast-bei-den-haus-frauen-16989018.html, accessed May 29, 2021.

2   Cf. Bundesarchitektenkammer, n.d.: Since 2006 the proportion of female graduates in architecture has been higher than 50 percent. Since then, it has steadily increased to 58 percent in 2019, dropping to 56 percent in 2020. In 2020 female graduates in interior design make up 86 percent, in landscape architecture 62 percent, and in spatial planning 58 percent. The Federal Chamber statistics have only been broken down by gender since 2001. The number of registered women architects are therefore only shown from 2001 onwards.

3   Cf. Architects' Council of Europe 2021: The proportion of women architects in Serbia is 67 percent, in Croatia 62 percent, and in Sweden and Poland 58 percent.

4   Cf. Architects' Council of Europe 2021.

5   Cf. Kaufmann/Ihsen/Villa Braslavsky 2018.

6   Williams/Korn/Maas 2021, 5.

7   Williams/Korn/Maas 2021, 3.

8   See Glossary.

9   Bundesarchitektenkammer 2020, 40–41. Italics in the original.

10   Kaufmann/Ihsen/Villa Braslavsky 2018, 31.

11   Cf. Kaufmann/Ihsen/Villa Braslavsky 2018, 38: A self-employed woman architect who runs her office together with a male partner, commented in an interview: "Even on the phone an incredible number of people have assumed I was the secretary. Although the studio bears my name and I answer the phone with my name ... . And that has really struck me quite often."

12   Cf. Marcus Fairs, "Survey of top architecture firms reveals 'quite shocking' lack of gender diversity at senior levels," *Dezeen*, November 16, 2017, https://www.dezeen.com/2017/11/16/survey-leading-architecture-firms-reveals-shocking-lack-gender-diversity-senior-levels/, accessed February 18, 2022.

13   Cf. Kaufmann/Ihsen/Villa Braslavsky 2018.

14   Baukultur Nordrhein-Westfalen. "Von der erfolgreichen Studentin zur unsichtbaren Architektin," September 23, 2020. Livestream. https://www.youtube.com/watch?v=E_9VH9uHSpA, accessed May 17, 2021.

15   Laurie Penny, "Laurie Penny on Feminism," Melbourne Writers Festival, https://www.youtube.com/watch?v=dE4-GbGXhJc, accessed February 21, 2022.

16   Cf. Schutzbach 2021.

17   Cf. Schutzbach 2021.

18   Cf. Allmendinger 2021, 52: Allmendinger explains that the marriage market is still more financially rewarding than the labor market. She cites the existing family policy incentive systems, such as spousal tax splitting and mini jobs, as reasons for this. If the couple divorces, the opposite occurs.

19   Allmendinger 2021, 19.

20   Cf. Bundesministerium für Familie, Senioren, Frauen und Jugend 2018, 12: "Women perform 52.4 percent more unpaid care work per day than men. This is equivalent to spending one hour and 27 minutes more each day."

21   Cf. Russell Hochschild/Machung 1989.

22   Cf. Cammarata 2020.

23   Cf. Bundesministerium für Familie, Senioren, Frauen und Jugend 2016.

24   Helene Klaar, "Im Gesetz steht von Liebe kein Wort," *Süd-deutsche Zeitung Magazin*, February 15, 2016: https://sz-magazin.sueddeutsche.de/liebe-und-partnerschaft/im-gesetz-steht-von-liebe-kein-wort-82190, accessed May 30, 2021.

25   Cf. Bundesministerium für Familie, Senioren, Frauen und Jugend 2016.

26   Cf. Laura Mark, *Architects Journal* (January 10, 2014), cit. in Stratigakos 2016, 27.

27   Williams/Korn/Maas 2021, 45.

28   Cf. Bruce Tether, "Results of the 2016 Women in Architecture Survey revealed," *Architectural Review*, February 26, 2016: https://www.architectural-review.com/essays/results-of-the-2016-women-in-architecture-survey-revealed, accessed February 16, 2022. According to the 2016 study by *Architects Journal* 75 percent of women architects do not have any children.

29   Cf. Kaufmann/Ihsen/Villa Braslavsky 2018; Schumacher 2004.

30   Cf. Architects' Council of Europe 2021: Women architects in Germany work an average of 42.6 hours a week, which is 3.8 hours more than in Denmark and 3.3 hours more than in Norway. Self-employed women architects in Germany work 50.1 hours per week, which is 10.3 hours longer than their female colleagues in Denmark, and 8.8 hours longer than their Norwegian colleagues.

31   Kern 2020, 5.

32   Cf. https://www.slowspace.org, accessed February 11, 2022.

33   Cf. Bund Deutscher Architektinnen und Architekten, "Frauen in der Architektur," *Podcast DenkLabor*, Episode 20.

34   Cf. Scott 2020, 167–69: Linda Scott outlines for the United States how free childcare for all American children would pay for itself to the tune of $84 billion by way of projected tax revenues of $271 billion. This assumes that women work as much as men.

35   Scott 2020, 13–14.

36   Cf. Scott 2020.

37   Scott 2020, 167.

38   Cf. Kaufmann/Ihsen/Villa Braslavsky 2018.

39   Cf. Weresch 2012.

40   Weresch 2012.

41   University of the West of England, July 3, 2003: https://info. uwe.ac.uk/news/uwenews/news.aspx?id=371, accessed February 10, 2022.

42   Stratigakos 2016, 71. Italics in the original.

43   Criado-Perez 2019, 24. Italics in the original.

44   Cf. Wikipedia Deutschland: https://de.wikipedia.org/wiki/Portal:Frauen/Biografien/Statistiken, accessed January 23, 2022.

45   Cf. Wikipedia Deutschland: https://de.wikipedia.org/wiki/Wikipedia:WikiProjekt_Frauen/Frauen_in_Rot, accessed January 23, 2022.

46   Cf. Wikipedia Deutschland: https://de.wikipedia.org/wiki/Wikipedia:WikiProjekt_Women_Wikipedia_Design/Startseite, accessed February 10, 2022.

47   Mary Pepchinski in a telephone conversation on January 27, 2022.

48   Cf. Dörhöfer 2004.

49   Dörhöfer 2004, 10.

50   Cf. Roig 2021.

51   Cf. Maasberg/Prinz 2012.

52   Dörhöfer 2004, 51.

53   Emilie Winkelmann, cit. in Klara Trost, "Die Frau als Architektin," *Die Frauenfachschule* 28 (1919), 569–72.

54   Cf. Eichhorn 2013.

55   Cf. Wikipedia Deutschland: https://de.wikipedia.org/wiki/Freibad_Letzigraben, accessed January 23, 2022.

56   Cf. Wikipedia Deutschland: https://de.wikipedia.org/wiki/Gertrud_Frisch-von_Meyenburg, accessed January 16, 2022.

57   Droste 2019, 40.

58   Maasberg/Prinz 2012, 639.

59   Cf. Scheffler 1908.

60   Dörhöfer 2004, 55.

61   Cf. Scott 2020.

62   Becky Anderson, December 8, 2012: https://edition.cnn.com/2012/08/01/business/leading-women-zaha-hadid/index.html, accessed May 26, 2021.

63   Kaiser 2021, 175.

64   Cf. Dörhöfer 2004.

65   Cf. Moholy-Nagy 1968.

66   Heynen 2019, 160.

67   Cf. Heynen 2019.

68   Cf. Colomina 2021a.

69   Oliver Koerner von Gustorf, June 9, 2015: https://www.style-park.com/de/news/die-rache-des-maschinisten, accessed March 6, 2022.

70   Cf. Colomina 2021b.

71   Cf. Colomina 2021b.

72   Cf. Beyerle/Nemecková 2019.

73   Cf. Scott Brown 1974.

74   Denise Scott Brown, cit. in Stratigakos 2016, 54.

75   Sara Ahmed, November 4, 2014: https://feministkilljoys.com/2014/11/04/white-men/, accessed January 23, 2022.

76   Cf. Fitz/Krasny 2019.

77   University College Dublin, April 22, 2021: https://www.ucd.ie/newsandopinion/news/2021/april/22/ercadvancedgrantforucdprojectexploringimpactofwomenandminoritiesonmodernarchitecture/, accessed January 17, 2022.

78   Dörhöfer 2004, 6.

79   de Jong 2012, 149.

80   Cf. Bolukbasi 2016.

81   Cf. Kaufmann/Ihsen/Villa Braslavsky 2018.

82   Justin Davidson, "Mr. & Mrs. Architect," *New York Magazine*, June 13, 2013, https://nymag.com/arts/architecture/features/architect-couples-2013-6/, accessed March 11, 2021.

83   Stratigakos 2016, 9.

84   Cf. de Graaf 2020.

85   Adey Siufan, "Live panel discussion with OMA's Reinier de Graaf about his novel The Masterplan," *Dezeen*, March 24, 2021, https://www.dezeen.com/2021/03/24/reiner-de-graaf-the-masterplan-live-talk/, accessed January 30, 2022.

86   Anonymous as told to Suzanne Labarre, "Exclusive: Why I star-

ted A 'Shitty Architecture Men' List," *Fast Company*, March 15, 2018, https://www.fastcompany.com/90164300/exclusive-why-i-started-a-shitty-architecture-men-list, accessed January 30, 2022.

87 Alexandra Lange, "The end of the architect profile," *Curbed*, April 19, 2018, https://www.alexandralange.net/articles/547/the-end-of-the-architect-profile, accessed January 30, 2022.

88 Mary Pepchinski, telephone conversation with the author on January 27, 2022.

89 Cf. Heynen 2012.

90 Cf. Volpp 2016.

91 Cf. Schumacher 2004.

92 Cf. Ihsen 2006, cit. in Volpp 2016, 11.

93 Schumacher 2004, 26.

94 Schumacher 2004, 22.

95 Cf. Manne 2019.

96 Schumacher 2004, 24.

97 Cf. Kaufmann/Ihsen/Villa Braslavsky 2018.

98 Dagmar Richter, cit. in Kullack 2011, 168–69.

99 Schumacher 2004, 22.

100 Cf. Toscano 2021.

101 Volpp 2016, 33.

102 Cf. Stratigakos 2016.

103 Hall 2019, 216.

104 Kaiser 2021, 160.

105 Cf. Manne 2019.

106 Williams/Korn/Maas 2021, 45.

107 Williams/Korn/Maas 2021, 12. Here, the authors of the study point to several investigations in further industries, such as Joan C. Williams, Marina Multhaup, Su Li, Rachel Korn, *You Can't Change What You Can't See: Interrupting Racial & Gender Bias in the Legal Profession,* 2018, American Bar Association & Minority Corporate Counsel Association: https://www.americanbar.org/content/dam/aba/administrative/women/you-cant-change-what-you-cant-see-print.pdf, accessed April 8, 2022.

108 Cathleen McGuigan, "January 2022 Editor's Letter: A Troubling Report on Bias in Architecture," *Architectural Record*, January 13, 2022, https://www.architecturalrecord.com/articles/15474-january-2022-editors-letter-a-troubling-report-on-bias-in-architecture, accessed February 12, 2022.

109 Océane Vé-Réveillac, cit. in Ulrike Sturm, "Nächstes Mal machen wir es besser falsch," *Bauwelt* 17 (2021): 37.

110 Cf. Neufert 2019.

111 Neufert 2019, vi.

112 Neufert 2019, vi.

113 These quotes concerning the alleged quality training of architecture students were taken from personal conversations with German professors of architecture.

114 Lange 2021.

115 Cf. Schumacher 2004.

116 Cf. Schumacher 2004.

117 Schumacher 2004, 15.

118 Technische Universität München, 2017, https://www.ar.tum.de/fakultaet/gleichstellung/forschung/umfrage-2017/, accessed May 29, 2021.

119 Stratigakos 2016, 22.

120 Cf. Technische Universität Wien, "Claiming Spaces: Feministische* Perspektiven in Architektur und Raumplanung, in *future.lab Magazin* 13 (2020).

121 Cf. Stratigakos 2016.

122 Cf. Kullack 2011.

123 Cf. Schwitalla 2021.

124 Wahlroos-Ritter, cit. in Kullack 2011, 172.

125 Cf. Schumacher 2004.

126 Cf. Ebert 2019.

127 This supervision took place in 2021 at a German university and was reported to the author in a personal conversation.

128 Stratigakos 2016, 23.

129 Cf. Ebert 2019.

130 Schumacher 2004, 15.

131 Jim Kunstler, "An interview with Jane Jacobs, Godmother of the American City," *Metropolis*, May 4, 2016, https://metropolismag. com/projects/jane-jacobs-godmother-of-the-american-city/, accessed February 16, 2022.

132 Cf. ARCH+ 2021.

133 See Glossary.

134 Cf. Kern 2020.

135 Cf. Kaufmann/Ihsen/Villa Braslavsky 2018.

136 Cf. Kern 2020.

137 Cf. Schnerring/Verlan 2020.

138 See Glossary.

139 Krasny 2019, 35.

140 Krasny 2019, 40.

141 Krasny 2019, 39.

142 Tronto 2019, 27.

143 Scott 2020, 14. "Men, as a group, often choose to spend money on their own indulgences, rather than sharing it with their families, even prioritizing expenditures on vices such as alcohol, tobacco, gambling, prostitution, and guns above their children's education."

144 Cf. Scott 2020, 11–17.

145 Anna Heringer, ACE Conference Climate Change & Built Heritage, October 28, 2021, https://www.youtube.com/watch?v= EU9SMSeiGIE&list=PLj-5oka8wwqsS0zvgrTv47bu1AuT7IO4y, accessed February 7, 2022.

146 Kern 2020, 16.

147 Cf. Christina Murray, "What would cities look like if they were designed by mothers?," *The Guardian*, August 27, 2018, https:// www.theguardian.com/commentisfree/2018/aug/27/architects-di- versity-cities-designed-mothers, accessed February 16, 2022.

148 Kern 2020, 41.

149 Kern 2020, 46.

150 Darke 1996, 88.

151 Cf. Jacobs 1961.

152 Cf. Anthony Paletta, "Story of cities #32: Jane Jacobs v Robert Moses, battle of New York's urban titans," *The Guardian*, April 28,

2016, https://www.theguardian.com/cities/2016/apr/28/story-cities-32-new-york-jane-jacobs-robert-moses, accessed February 17, 2022.

153 Cf. *A Marvelous Order* (2021), http://mosesjacobsopera.com, accessed May 1, 2021.

154 Cf. Jacobs 2019.

155 Kern 2020, 154–55.

156 Cf. The City of Copenhagen, *Architecture Policy for Copenhagen 2017–2025. Architecture for People*. 2017.

157 Cf. Morgane Llanque, "Wie sich Paris neu erfindet," *enorm*, September 6, 2021, https://enorm-magazin.de/gesellschaft/urbanisierung/wie-sich-paris-neu-erfindet, accessed February 17, 2022.

158 Cf. Sadik-Khan 2017.

159 Amazon (n.d.), https://www.amazon.de/Streetfight-Handbook-Revolution-Janette-Sadik-Khan/dp/0143128973, accessed February 17, 2022.

160 "Green Guerillas," Wikipedia United States, https://en.wikipedia.org/wiki/Green_Guerillas, accessed February 17, 2022.

161 Cf. Liz Christy Community Garden, http://lizchristygarden.us, accessed February 17, 2022.

162 Cf. Col·lectiu Punt 6 2019, Muxí Martínez 2021.

163 Cf. Bilbao 2022.

164 Cf. FEMPUBLICBCN, https://www.bcnuej.org/projects/fempublicbcn/, accessed February 17, 2022.

165 *La Ciudad Amable* means "the friendly city" in English.

166 See Glossary.

167 Cf. Tina Groll, "Wir müssen das Dorf zurück in die Stadt bringen," *Zeit Online*, February 13, 2021, https://www.zeit.de/mobilitaet/2021-02/stadtplanung-wien-eva-kail-gender-planning-frauen, accessed February 17, 2022.

168 Cf. Stadt Wien, "Geschlechtssensible Verkehrsplanung," https://www.wien.gv.at/stadtentwicklung/alltagundfrauen/pdf/verkehr-la.pdf.

169 Petra Unger, 2021, cit. in Wojciech Cjaja, *Bauwelt* 17 (2021): 35; Wiener Frauen*Spaziergänge, https://frauenspaziergaenge.at, accessed March 6, 2022.

170   Cf. Zibell/Damyanovic/Sturm 2019.

171   Cf. European Institute for Gender Equality, "Gender Mainstreaming: Gender planning," December 13, 2018, https://eige.europa.eu/publications/gender-mainstreaming-gender-planning, accessed January 17, 2021.

172   Cf. Zibell/Damyanovic/Sturm 2019.

173   The Institute of Architecture and Technology, KADK Copenhagen published the two-volume *An Architecture Guide to the UN 17 Sustainable Development Goals*, see: https://uia2023cph.org/the-guides, accessed February 18, 2022.

174   Cf. The World Bank, "Handbook for Gender-Inclusive Urban Planning and Design," February 4, 2020, https://www.worldbank.org/en/topic/urbandevelopment/publication/handbook-for-gender-inclusive-urban-planning-and-design, accessed February 18, 2022.

175   Kern 2020, 63.

176   "Vigils," Reclaim These Streets, accessed February 6, 2022, https://reclaimthesestreets.com/vigils/.

177   See Glossary.

178   Katie Falkingham, "Reclaim These Streets: Female athletes share experiences of training alone," BBC Sport, March 14, 2021: https://www.bbc.com/sport/athletics/56392440, accessed May 20, 2022.

179   Carla Baum, Fiona Weber-Steinhaus, Tülay Karakus, and Julia Meyer, "Would someone hear me if I had to yell for help?", *Die ZEIT*, March 18, 2021: https://www.zeit.de/zeit-magazin/2021-03/sexismus-frauen-joggen-cat-calling-belaestigung-angst-erfahrung, accessed March 27, 2021.

180   Safe & the City, https://safeandthecity.com, accessed March 27, 2021.

181   Safe & the City, accessed February 6, 2022.

182   Cf. "Public spaces need to be safe and inclusive for all. Now." United Nations Women, https://www.unwomenuk.org/safe-spaces-now, accessed June 21, 2021.

183   Kern 2020, 158.

184   Kern 2020, 147–48.

185 Cf. Kern 2020.

186 Cf. Scott 2020.

187 Cf. Löw 2016.

188 Löw 2016, 210–11.

189 Löw 2016, 211.

190 Cf. Löw 2016.

191 Cf. "Girls Design the Reumannplatz," Lokale Agenda 21 Wien, https://www.agendafavoriten.at/projekte-detail/maedchen-gestalten-den-reumannplatz-p.html, accessed March 6, 2022.

192 Cf. Fröbe 2020.

193 "FLICKRUM—Places for girls," White Arkitekter, https://whitearkitekter.com/project/places-for-girls/, accessed February 18, 2022.

194 Monica Ponce de Leon, cit. in Kullack 2011, 167.

195 Stratigakos 2016, 26.

196 Cf. Budde et al 2017.

197 Cf. Schumacher 2004.

198 Stratigakos 2016, 66.

199 Matthias Hennies, *Deutschlandfunk*, March 25, 2021, https://www.deutschlandfunk.de/aus-kultur-und-sozialwissenschaften.1147.de.html, accessed March 26, 2021.

200 Cf. Schutzbach 2018.

201 Cf. Kunekath 2021.

202 Cf. Roig 2021. Emilia Roig speaks about four different dimensions of discrimination which are mutually dependent and reinforce one another: individual, structural, institutional, and historical discrimination (see Glossary). From the definition, the discrimination of privileged groups does not go beyond individual discrimination, as it has no systematic foundation and corresponding impact.

203 Cf. Wolfgang Thierse, "Ziemlich demokratiefremd," 25 February, 2021, https://www.deutschlandfunk.de/wolfgang-thierse-spd-ueber-identitaetspolitik-ziemlich-100.html, accessed February 25, 2022.

204 Cf. *Deutsches Architektenblatt*, no. 4 (2021).

205 Christian Gesellmann, "Wir sollten uns schämen," *Die Zeit*, March 22, 2021, https://www.zeit.de/zeit-magazin/leben/2021-03/

femismus-sexismus-mordfall-sarah-everard-belaestigung-maenner, accessed May 5, 2021.

206 Maasberg/Prinz 2012.

207 Cf. Bundesministerium für Umwelt, Naturschutz, Bau und Reaktorsicherheit (ed.), Richtlinie für Planungswettbewerbe – RPW 2013: https://www.bmi.bund.de/SharedDocs/downloads/DE/veroeffentlichungen/2013/richtlinie-planungswettbewerbe.pdf?__blob=publicationFile&v=2, accessed March 6, 2022.

208 "Manifesto," Architecture Lobby, http://architecture-lobby.org/about/, accessed February 19, 2022.

209 These observations stem from professional experiences made by the author in the area of supervising competitions over a period of fifteen years.

210 Senatsverwaltung für Stadtentwicklung, "Gender Mainstreaming in der Stadtentwicklung," https://www.stadtentwicklung.berlin.de/soziale_stadt/gender_mainstreaming/download/gender_deutsch.pdf, accessed February 19, 2022.

211 Zentrum Frau in Beruf und Technik, https://www.zfbt.de/veroeffentlichungen/dokumente/planungswettbewerbe.pdf, accessed February 19, 2022.

212 Cf. Stadtentwicklung Wien 2013.

213 Cf. Schwitalla 2021.

214 Cf. W Awards, https://w-awards.architectural-review.com/wprog/en/page/about, accessed February 17, 2021.

215 Cf. "Prize 2021," femmes architects, https://www.femmes-archi.org/en/prize-2021/, accessed February 18, 2021.

216 Stratigakos 2016, 63.

217 Cf. Zibell/Karácsony 2018.

218 Cf. ARCH+ 2021.

219 Lange 2021.

220 Cf. ARCH+ 2021.

221 de Jong 2021.

222 Cf. Lorde 1984.

223 Cf. Lorde 1984.

224 Joan C. Tronto and Berenice Fisher, 1990, cit. in Tronto 2019, 29. Italics in the original.

225 Cf. Roig 2021.

226 "What is Intersectionality," Center for Intersectional Justice, https://www.intersectionaljustice.org/what-is-intersectionality, accessed March 23, 2022.

227 Anna von Rath and Lucy Gasser, "10 Terms Related to Identities that Require Sensitivity in Translation," Goethe-Institut, February 2021, https://www.goethe.de/prj/one/en/aco/art/22106971.html, accessed April 22, 2022.

228 Nadia Shehadeh, "Huh? What does privilege mean?", *Missy Magazine*, 8 January 2017, https://missy-magazine.de/blog/2017/08/01/hae-was-heisst-denn-privilegien/, accessed March 23, 2022. Italics in the original.

229 "Rape culture," Europäisches Institut für Gleichstellungsfragen (EIGE) European Institute for Gender Equality (EIGE), https://eige.europa.eu/thesaurus/terms/1341, accessed March 23, 2022.

230 Illgner 2018, 264.

231 Cf. Illgner 2018.

Bibliography

Allmendinger, Jutta. *Es geht nur gemeinsam: Wie wir endlich Geschlechtergerechtigkeit erreichen*. Berlin: Ullstein, 2021.

ARCH+ 54, no. 246, "Zeitgenössische feministische Raumpraxis" (2021).

Architects' Council of Europe. *The Architectural Profession in Europe 2020: A Sector Study*. Brussels, 2021.

Bauwelt, no. 17, "Gendergerechte Architektur" (2021).

Beyerle, Tulga, and Klara Nemecková, eds. *Gegen die Unsichtbarkeit: Designerinnen der Deutschen Werkstätten Hellerau 1898 bis 1938*. Dresden: Hirmer, 2019.

Bilbao, Tatiana, "Stadt der Fürsorge / City of Care," *Die Architekt* 1 (2022): 20–24.

Bolukbasi, Tolga et al., *Man is to Computer Programmer as Woman is to Homemaker? Debiasing Word Embeddings*, arXiv:1607.06520v1 [cs.CL]. Boston and Cambridge, MA: 2016.

Budde, Christina, Mary Pepchinski, Peter Cachola Schmal, and Wolfgang Voigt, eds. *Frau Architekt: Seit mehr als 100 Jahren Frauen im Architektenberuf / Over 100 Years of Women as Professional Architects*. Berlin: Wasmuth & Zohlen, 2017.

Bundesarchitektenkammer. "Aktuelle Zahlen Absolventinnen und Absolventen," n.d. https://bak.de/politik-und-praxis/wirtschaft-und-mittelstand/ausbildung-aktuelle-zahlen-studierende/#absolventin-nen-und-absolventen, accessed March 3, 2022.

Bundesarchitektenkammer. "Geschlechtsspezifische Gehaltsunterschie-de bei angestellten Kammermitgliedern: Eine Sonderauswertung der Daten der bundesweiten Strukturbefragung der Architektenkammern der Länder im Jahr 2020," 2020. https://bak.de/wp-content/up-loads/2021/02/2020_bak_strukturbefragung_sonderbericht-gehalts-unterschiede-nach-geschlecht_2021.pdf, accessed March 3, 2022.

Bundesministerium für Familie, Senioren, Frauen und Jugend, ed. *Mitten im Leben: Wünsche und Lebenswirklichkeiten von Frauen zwi-schen 30 und 50 Jahren*. Berlin, 2016.

Bundesministerium für Familie, Senioren, Frauen und Jugend, ed. *Mitten im Leben. Wünsche und Lebenswirklichkeiten von Frauen zwi-schen 30 und 50 Jahren*. Berlin, 2016.

Bundesministerium für Familie, Senioren, Frauen und Jugend, ed. *Zweiter Gleichstellungsbericht der Bundesregierung*. Berlin, 2018.

Cammarata, Patricia. *Raus aus der Mental Load-Falle: Wie gerechte Arbeitsteilung in der Familie gelingt*. Weinheim and Basel: Beltz GmbH, 2020.

Col·lectiu Punt 6. *Urbanismo Feminista*. Barcelona: Virus Editorial, 2019.

Colomina, Beatriz as told to Katarina Bonnevier: "Die Architekturge-schichte gegen den Strich bürsten," in: *ARCH+* 246 (2021a): 116–23.

Colomina, Beatriz: "Eileen Gray. E.1027," in: Schwittala, Ursula, ed. *Women in Architecture: Past, Present and Future*. Ostfildern:

Hatje Cantz Verlag 2021b, 34–41.

Criado-Perez, Caroline. *Invisible Women: Exposing Data Bias in a World designed for Men*. London: Vintage, 2019.

Darke, Jane. "The Man-Shaped City." In *Changing Places: Women's Lives in the City,* ed. by Christine Booth, Jane D. Darke, and Susan Yeandle. London: Sage Publishing, 1996, 88–99.

Dörhöfer, Kerstin. *Pionierinnen in der Architektur: Eine Baugeschichte der Moderne*. Tübingen and Berlin: Wasmuth & Zohlen, 2004.

Droste, Magdalena, *Das Bauhaus 1919–1933*. Cologne: Taschen Verlag, 2019.

Ebert, Carola. "Inseln der Selbstreflexion: Drei Debatten zur Architekturlehre im 21. Jahrhundert." In *Forum Architekturwissenschaft*. Vol. 3, *Vom Baumeister zum Master: Formen der Architekturlehre vom 19. bis ins 21. Jahrhundert*, ed. by Carola Ebert, Eva Maria Froschauer, and Christiane Salge. Berlin, 2019, 424–42.

Eichhorn, Ulrike. *Architektinnen: Ihr Beruf. Ihr Leben*. Berlin: fembooks, 2013.

Fitz, Angelika, and Elke Krasny, eds. *Critical Care: Architecture and Urbanism for a Broken Planet*. Vienna: Architekturzentrum Wien/ Cambridge, MA, and London: The MIT Press, 2019.

Fröbe, Turit, *Architectural Policy in Finland: Architecture as Civic Education*. Berlin: JOVIS Verlag, 2020.

de Graaf, Reinier. *The Masterplan: A Novel*. Amsterdam: Archis, 2020.

Hall, Jane. *Breaking Ground: Architecture by Women*. London and New York: Phaidon, 2019.

Heynen, Hilde. "Genius, Gender and Architecture: The Star System as Exemplified in the Pritzker Price." *Architectural Theory Review* 17, nos. 2–3 (2012), 331–45, DOI 10.1080/13264826.2012.727443, accessed March 2, 2021.

Heynen, Hilde. *Sibyl Moholy-Nagy: Kritikerin der Moderne*. Dresden: Sandstein, 2019.

Illgner, Johannah Lea. "Hass-Kampagnen und Silencing im Netz," in *Antifeminismus in Bewegung: Aktuelle Debatten um Geschlecht und sexuelle Vielfalt*, ed. by Juliane Lang and Ulrich Peters. Hamburg: Marta Press, 2018, 253–72.

Jacobs, Jane. *Death and Life of Great American Cities*. New York: Random House, 1961.

Jacobs, Jane. *Cuatro Entrevistas*. Barcelona: Editorial Gustavo Gili, 2019.

de Jong, Afaina. *For the People by the People: A Visual Story of the DIY City*. Amsterdam: Ultra de la Rue Publishing, 2012.

de Jong, Afaina. "Ein Brief an Audre Lorde," *ARCH+: Zeitgenössische feministische Raumpraxis* 54, no. 246 (December 2021): 166–67.

Kaiser, Mareice. *Das Unwohlsein der modernen Mutter.* Hamburg: Rowohlt Verlag, 2021.

Kaufmann, Hermann, Susanne Ihsen, and Paula-Irene Villa Braslavsky. *Frauen in der Architektur*. Munich, 2018.

Kern, Leslie. *Feminist City: Claiming Space in a Man-Made World*. London and New York: Verso, 2020.

Krasny, Elke. "Architecture and Care," in Fitz, Angelika, and Elke

Krasny. *Critical Care: Architecture and Urbanism for a Broken Planet*. Vienna: Architekturzentrum Wien/Cambridge, MA, and London: The MIT Press, 2019, 33–41.

Kullack, Tanja, ed. *Architecture: A Woman's Profession*. Berlin: JOVIS Verlag, 2011.

Kunekath, Kerstin. "Die neuen Chefinnen." In *Deutsches Architekten-blatt* 2 (2021): 12–20.

Lange, Torsten. "Von der Schief- in die Schräglage kommen," *Bau-welt* 17 (2021): 20–21.

Lorde, Audre. *Sister Outsider: Essays and Speeches*. Toronto: Crossing Press, 1984.

Löw, Martina. *The Sociology of Space: Materiality, Social Structures and Action*. New York: Palgrave Macmillan, 2016.

Maasberg, Ute, and Regine Prinz. "Aller Anfang sind wir: Wege von Architektinnen im 20. Jahrhundert." In *Der Architekt: Geschichte und Gegenwart eines Berufsstandes,* ed. by Winfried Nerdinger. Munich: Prestel Verlag, 2012, 635–51.

Manne, Kate. *Down Girl: The Logic of Misogyny*. New York: Oxford University Press, 2019.

Moholy-Nagy, Sibyl. *Matrix of Man: An Illustrated History of Urban Environment*. Westport, CT: Praeger, 1968.

Muxí Martínez, Zaida: *Beyond the Threshold. Women, houses, and cities*. Barcelona: dpr-Barcelona, 2021.

Neufert, Ernst. *Bauentwurfslehre*. Wiesbaden: Springer Vieweg Verlag, 2019.

Roig, Emilia. *Why we matter: Das Ende der Unterdrückung*. Berlin: Aufbau Verlag, 2021.

Russell Hochschild, Arlie, and Anne Machung, *The Second Shift: Working Parents and the Revolution at Home*. New York: Viking, 1989.

Sadik-Khan, Janette. *Streetfight: Handbook for an Urban Revolution*. New York: Penguin Books, 2017.

Scheffler, Karl. *Die Frau und die Kunst: Eine Studie*. Berlin: J. Bard, 1908.

Schnerring, Almut, and Sascha Verlan, *Equal Care: Über Fürsorge und Gesellschaft*. Leck: 2020.

Schumacher, Christina. *Zur Unterverteilung von Frauen im Architekturberuf*. Forum Bildung und Beschäftigung. Schweizerische Koordinationsstelle für Bildungsforschung. Bern and Aarau, 2004.

Schutzbach, Franziska. *Die Rhetorik der Rechten: Rechtspopulistische Diskursstrategien im Überblick*. Zurich: Xanthippe, 2018.

Schutzbach, Franziska. *Die Erschöpfung der Frauen: Wider die weibliche Verfügbarkeit*. Munich: Droemer HC, 2021.

Schwitalla, Ursula, ed. *Women in Architecture: Past, Present and Future*. Ostfildern: Hatje Cantz Verlag, 2021.

Scott, Linda. *The Double X Economy: The Epic Potential of Women's Empowerment*. London: Faber & Faber, 2020.

Scott Brown, Denise. "Room at the Top? Sexism and the Star System in Architecture," in *Architecture: A Place for Women*, ed. by Ellen Perry Berkeley and Matilda McQuaid. Washington, DC: Smithsonian Institution Press, 1989, 237–46.

Stadtentwicklung Wien, ed. "Gender Mainstreaming in der Stadtplanung und Stadtentwicklung." *Werkstattberichte*, no. 130. Vienna, 2013.

Stratigakos, Despina. *Where Are the Women Architects?* Princeton and Oxford: Princeton University Press, 2016.

Toscano, Inés, "'Gender Masquerade' von architektonischen Paarungen," *Bauwelt* 17 (2021), 38–39.

Tronto, Joan C.: "Caring Architecture," in Fitz, Angelika, and Elke Krasny. *Critical Care: Architecture and Urbanism for a Broken Planet.* Vienna: Architekturzentrum Wien/Cambridge, MA, and London: The MIT Press, 2019, 26–32.

Volpp, Rebecca. *Architektinnen der Zukunft: Frauen hinterfragen den Habitus einer Profession.* Norderstedt: GRIN Verlag, 2016.

Weresch, Katharina. "Rund um die Uhr gefordert. Frauen in der Architektur." *Deutsches Architektenblatt*, November 1, 2012. https://www.dabonline.de/2012/11/01/rund-um-die-uhr-gefordert/.

Williams, Joan C., Rachel M. Korn, and Rachel Maas for The American Institute of Architects and The Center for WorkLife Law, eds. *The Elephant in the (Well-Designed) Room: An Investigation into Bias in the Architecture Profession.* Washington, DC, 2021.

Zibell, Barbara, Doris Damyanovic, and Ulrike Sturm, eds. *Gendered Approaches to Spatial Development in Europe: Perspectives, Similarities, Differences.* London: Routledge, 2019.

Zibell, Barbara, and Maya Karácsony, eds. *Frauennetzwerke in Architektur & Planung: Erfahrungen, Orientierungen.* Zurich: Hochparterre, 2018.

Acknowledgments

I would like to thank all of my conversation partners for sharing valuable information and their time with me. I am indebted to Afaina de Jong for agreeing to be interviewed on trains and train station platforms in the Netherlands. I would especially like to thank my German copy editor, Nicole Mahne, as well as Theresa Hartherz, Doris Kleilein and the entire team at JOVIS Verlag. Joann Skrypzak-Davidsmeyer and Rebecca van Dyck translated the book into English, and Ute Hasekamp translated the English portions into German, for which I am grateful. A big shoutout goes to Monika Grobel-Jaroschewski (PAPINESKA) for her lovely book design. She succeeded in lending the volume's complex subject matter a fitting graphic form within a short amount of time. My thanks also go to my close friends and to Johanna—you contributed significantly to making *Black Turtleneck, Round Glasses* a thought, an idea, and ultimately a book. My deepest gratitude goes to my children, Lorenz, Leonhard, and Konrad.

Image Credits

Fig. 1: Infographic showing women graduates in architecture versus registered women architects 1995–2020
Source: Federal Chamber of German Architects/Federal Statistical Office of Germany H201/Kaufmann/Ihsen/Villa Braslavsky 2018/Analysis: Karin Hartmann/Infographic: PAPINESKA
Caption: Women graduates in architecture versus registered women architects 1995–2020

Fig. 2: Unconscious biases
Source: Sarah Cooper/Square Peg London
Caption: The same statements made by women and men can be interpreted differently

Fig. 3: Infographic showing the gender balance in the architecture offices listed in the BauNetz Top 100 national ranking
Source: BauNetz Top 100 national ranking, January 2021/Analysis: Karin Hartmann/Infographic: PAPINESKA
Caption: Gender balance in German architecture offices listed in the BauNetz Top 100 national ranking

Fig. 4: Infographic: Biographies of women architects in Wikipedia
Source: Wikipedia Deutschland/Analysis: Karin Hartmann/Infographic: PAPINESKA
Caption: The share of female biographies in contrast to the biographies of female architects on Wikipedia Deutschland

Fig. 5: Statement by Susanne Gross
Source: Claudia Dreyße
Caption: Statement made by Susanne Gross on the occasion of the exhibition "Frau Architekt" in North Rhine-Westphalia in November 2020

Fig. 6: Le Corbusier painting the murals in E.1027
Source: Fondation Le Corbusier/VG Bild-Kunst Bonn
Caption: Le Corbusier had himself photographed in the nude while painting the murals in E.1027

Fig. 7: Infographic: Women professors in architecture 2005–20
Source: Federal Statistical Office of Germany/Analysis: Karin Hartmann/Infographic: PAPINESKA
Caption: Women professors and visiting professors in architecture in Germany in 2005–20

Fig. 8: Floor plan of the house designed by Marlene Poelzig
Source: Scan from *Bauwelt* 1930, no. 34
Caption: Floor plan of the house designed by Marlene Poelzig, Berlin-Westend

Fig. 9: Urbanismo Feminista
Source: María del Mar Muriel
Caption: The Caring City—La Ciudad Cuidadora

Fig. 10: Clips from the opera in Times Square
Source: Ka-Man Tse
Caption: Clips from the opera *A Marvelous Order* on the digital monitors in Times Square, New York City

Fig. 11: Community Garden in Alphabet City, 2015
Source: Karin Hartmann
Caption: Community Garden in Alphabet City on the Lower East Side

Fig. 12: Jane-Jacobs-Weg and Janis-Joplin-Promenade
Source: Karin Hartmann
Caption: Jane-Jacobs-Weg and Janis-Joplin-Promenade in the Seestadt Aspern district of Vienna

Fig. 13: Reumannplatz
Source: Karin Hartmann
Caption: Gender-inclusive Reumannplatz in Vienna

Fig. 14: Infographic: Women in specialist architectural journals
Source: Analysis: Karin Hartmann/Infographic: PAPINESKA
Caption: Depiction of women and men with a share of women authors in specialist architectural journals in 2016 and 2021/22

Fig. 15: Poster for the Parity Talks III 2018
Source: Parity Group/Original Photo Courtesy OMA, Design by Völlm+Walthert
Caption: Poster for the Parity Talks III 2018

Fig. Front inside cover: Reumannplatz, Vienna
Source: Karin Hartmann
Caption: Reumannplatz in Vienna, also known as Reumädchenplatz